Collins

KS2 Maths & English

SATs 10 Minute Tests

Jon Goulding

How to Use this Book

This book consists of maths and English tests for Key Stage 2, covering all the papers children will take in the Key Stage 2 SATs tests. Each test is designed to be completed in approximately 10 minutes.

This book contains:

- 8 Maths Arithmetic tests
- 8 Maths Reasoning tests
- 8 English Reading tests
- 8 English Grammar and Punctuation tests
- 8 English Spelling tests

Consisting of SATs-style questions in bite-sized chunks, each 10-minute test will help children to prepare for the Key Stage 2 SATs papers at home.

Clearly laid out questions and easy-to-use answers will help your child become familiar with, and gain confidence in, answering and understanding SATs-style questions.

The tests are all the same level of difficulty, which means they can be carried out in any order and at any time throughout Year 6 to provide invaluable practice for your child.

Children should work in a quiet environment where they can complete each test undisturbed. They should complete each test in approximately 10 minutes.

The number of marks available for each question is given on the right-hand side of the test pages, with a total provided at the end of each test.

For the Spelling tests, you will need to help your child by reading out the words they are required to spell. Instructions are given in the Answers section on page 125.

Answers and marking guidance are provided for each test. A score chart can be found at the back of the book, which your child can use to record their marks and see their progress.

Acknowledgements

The author and publisher are grateful to the copyright holders for permission to use quoted materials and images.

Images are © Shutterstock.com and © HarperCollins*Publishers*

Every effort has been made to trace copyright holders and obtain their permission for the use of copyright material. The author and publisher will gladly receive information enabling them to rectify any error or omission in subsequent editions. All facts are correct at time of going to press.

Published by Collins
An imprint of HarperCollins*Publishers*
1 London Bridge Street
London SE1 9GF

HarperCollins*Publishers*
Macken House, 39/40 Mayor Street Upper,
Dublin 1, D01 C9W8, Ireland

ISBN: 9780008335908

Content first published 2019
This edition published 2020
Previously published by Letts

10 9 8 7

British Library Cataloguing in Publication Data.

A CIP record of this book is available from the British Library.

Author: Jon Goulding
Commissioning Editors: Michelle I'Anson and Fiona McGlade
Editor and Project Manager: Katie Galloway
Cover Design: Kevin Robbins and Sarah Duxbury
Inside Concept Design: Ian Wrigley
Text Design and Layout: Jouve India Private Limited
Production: Karen Nulty
Printed and bound in the UK

Contents

Arithmetic Test 1

10 min

1 $2 \times 5 \times 20 =$

1 mark

2 $\frac{32}{50} - \frac{18}{50} =$

1 mark

3 $\square \times 8 = 96$

1 mark

4 40% of $2,100 =$

1 mark

5 $8 \times 4.25 =$

1 mark

6 $\square + 1,000 - 350 = 1,420$

1 mark

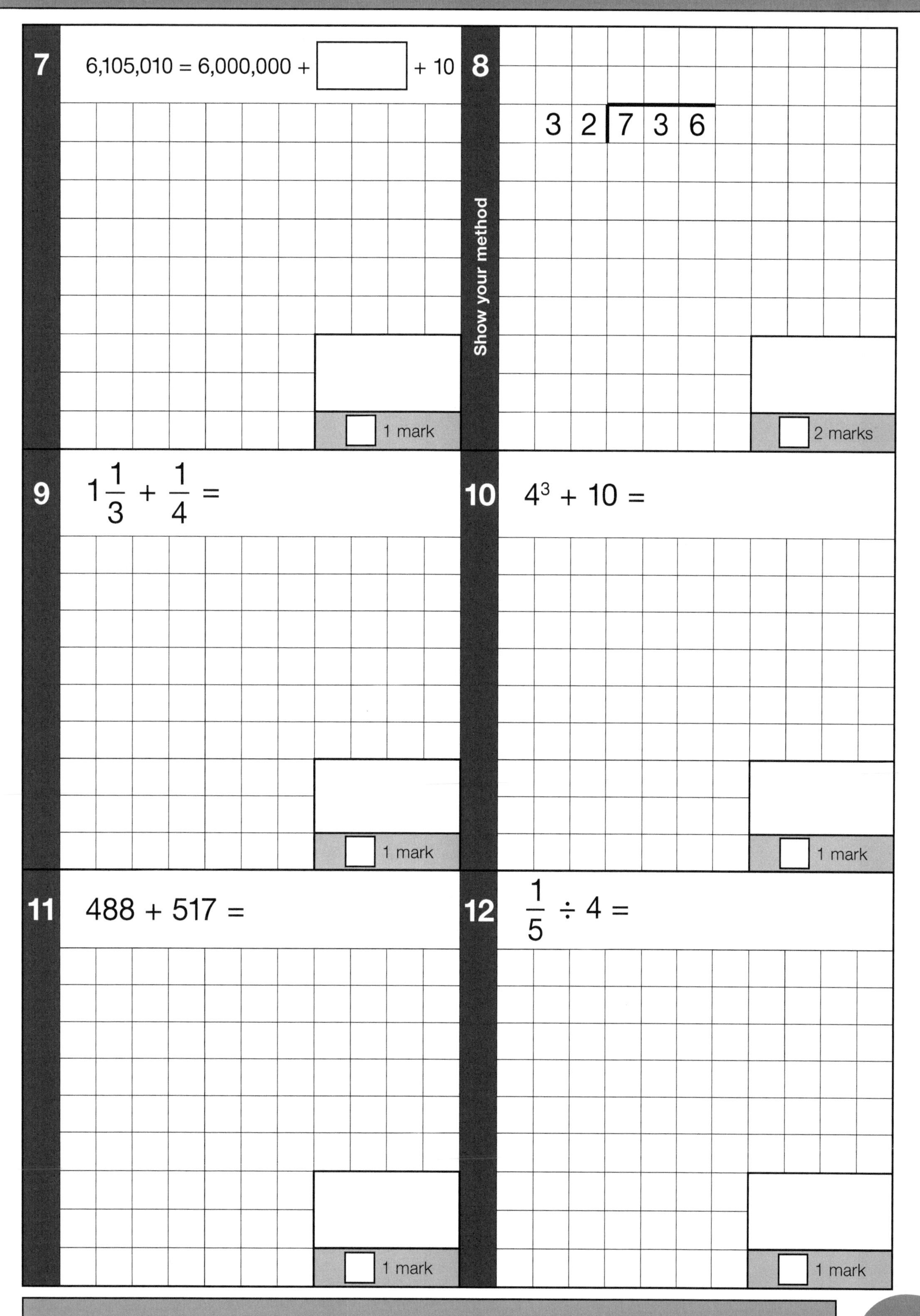

7 $6{,}105{,}010 = 6{,}000{,}000 + \square + 10$

1 mark

8 Show your method

$32\overline{)736}$

2 marks

9 $1\frac{1}{3} + \frac{1}{4} =$

1 mark

10 $4^3 + 10 =$

1 mark

11 $488 + 517 =$

1 mark

12 $\frac{1}{5} \div 4 =$

1 mark

Test 1 total marks ..../13

Arithmetic Test 2

10 min

1. $\square + 100 = 4{,}503$

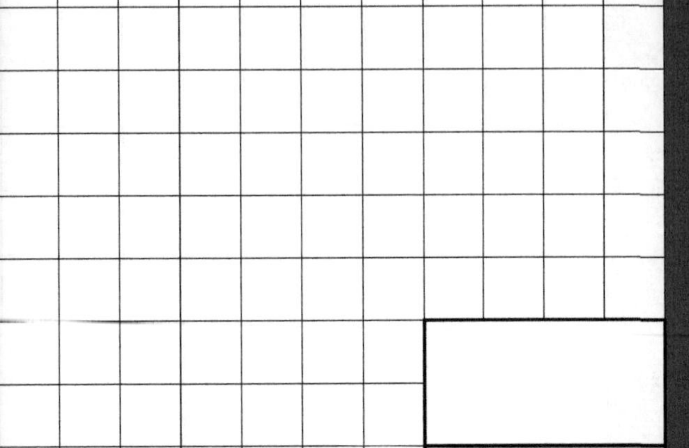

1 mark

2. $\frac{10}{12} - \frac{3}{12} =$

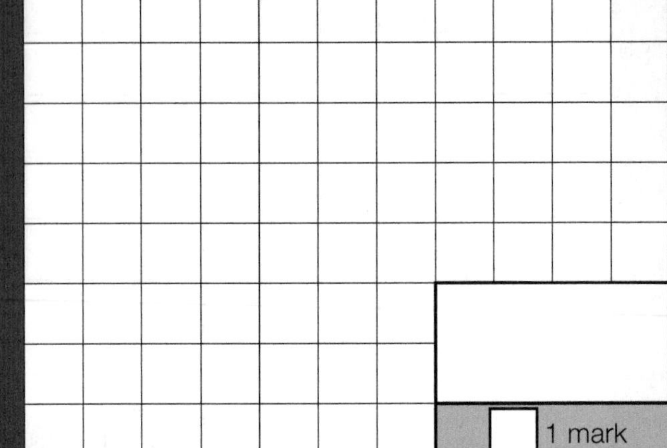

1 mark

3. $3.42 \times 4 =$

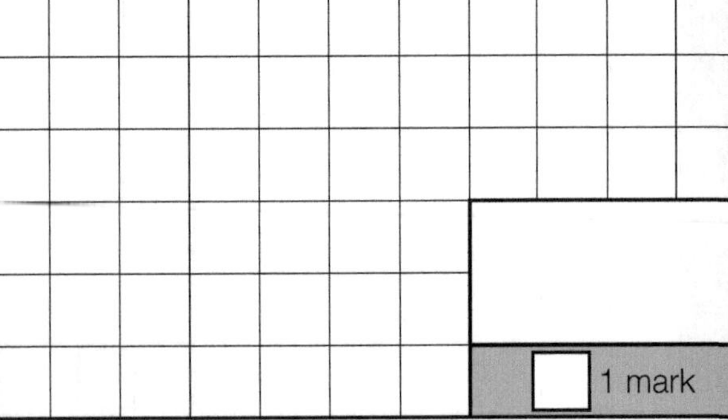

1 mark

4. $\frac{3}{18} + \frac{4}{6} =$

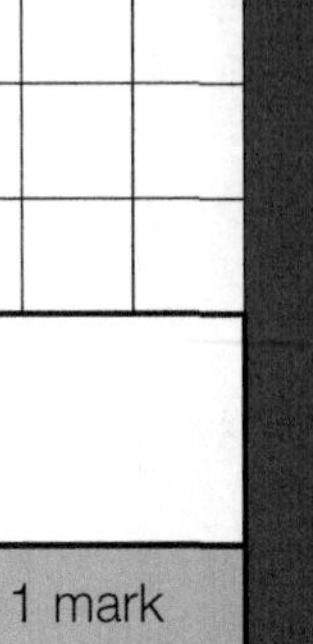

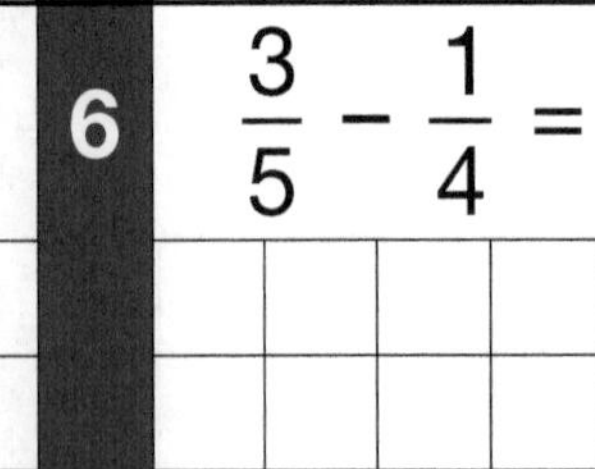

1 mark

5. $608 \div 8 =$

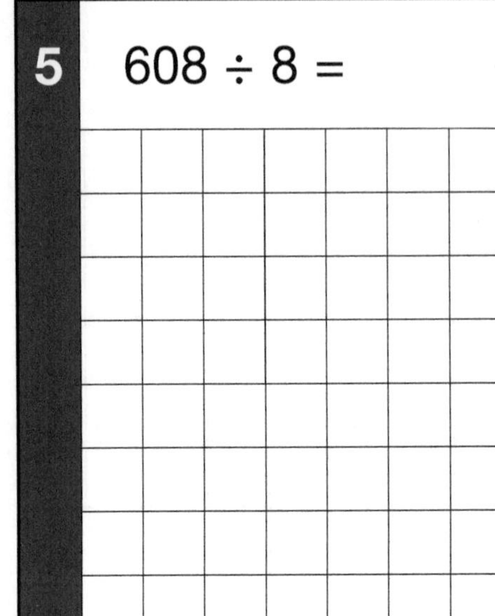

1 mark

6. $\frac{3}{5} - \frac{1}{4} =$

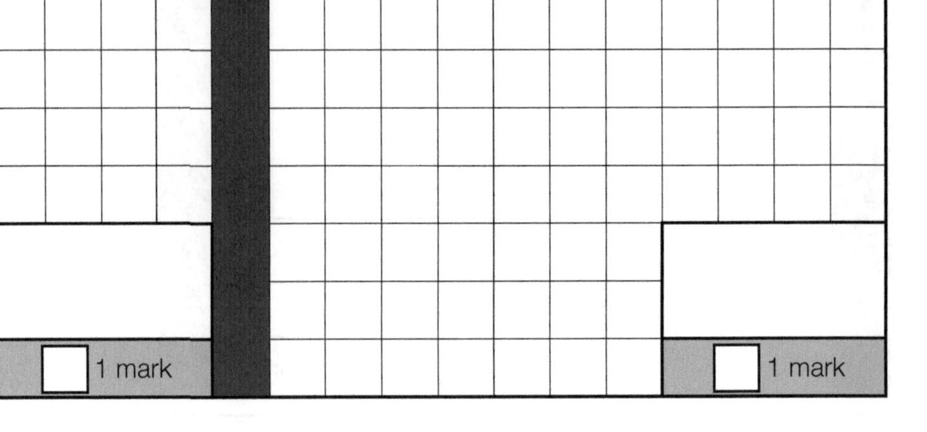

1 mark

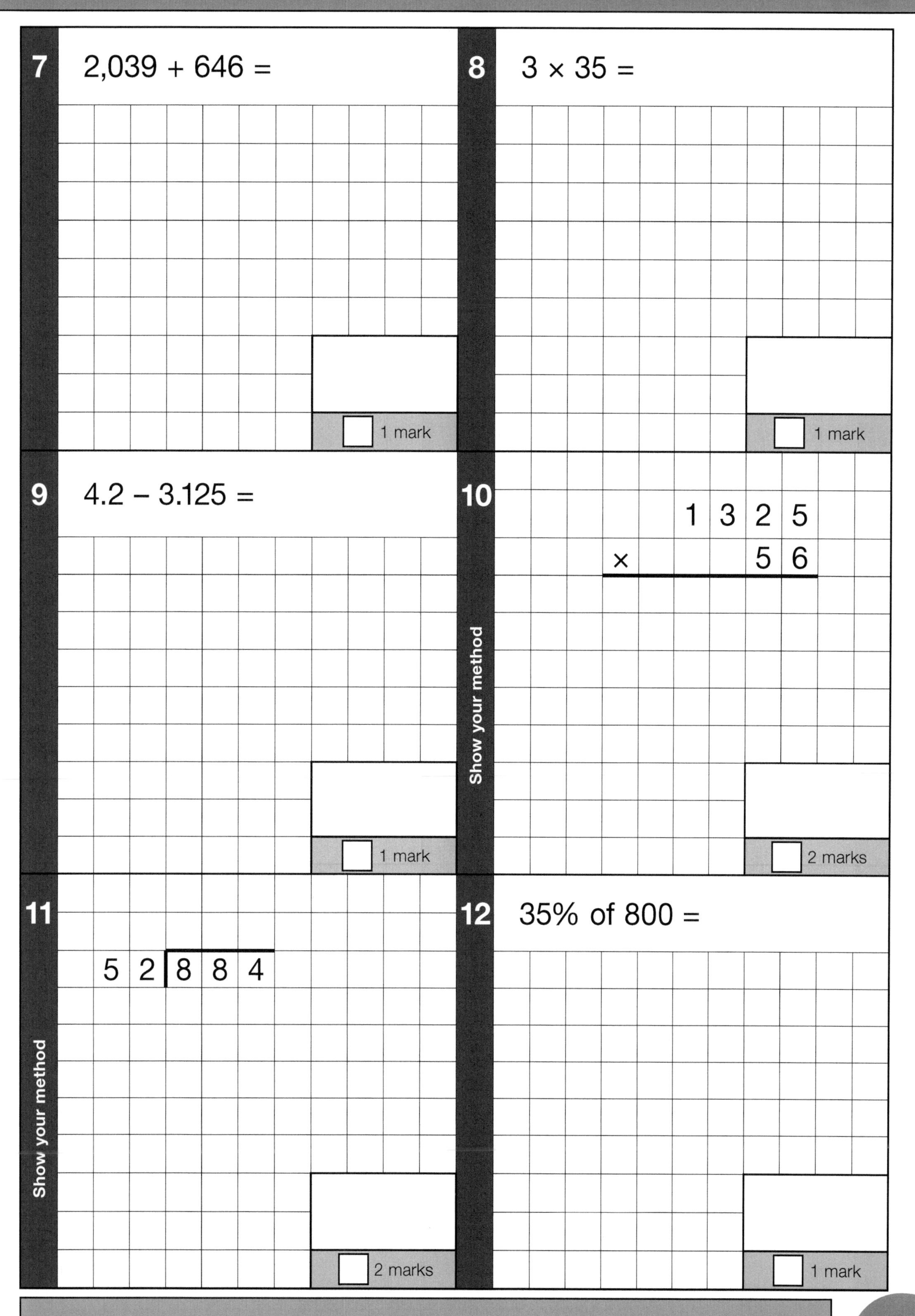

Test 2 total marks ..../14

Arithmetic Test 3

10 min

1 $12 \times 1 \times 6 =$

2 $9{,}782 - \square = 8{,}782$

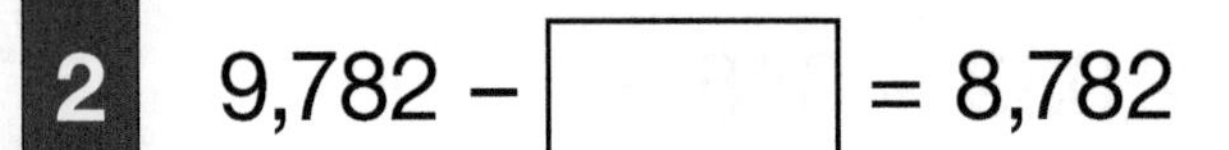

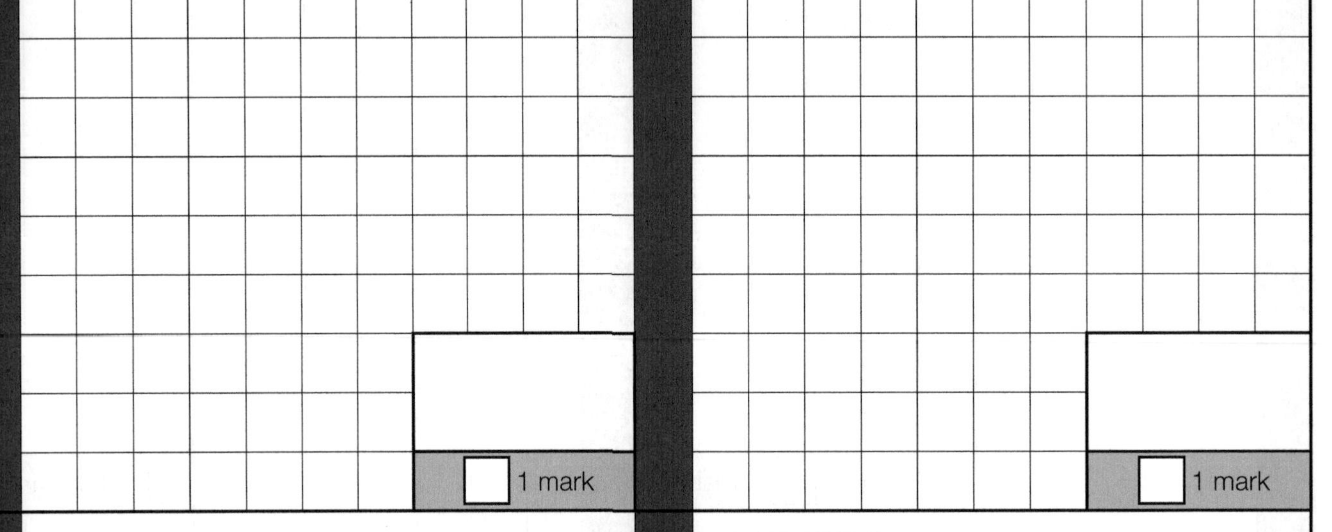

1 mark

1 mark

3 $263 \times 7 =$

4 $\square + 2.35 = 7.5$

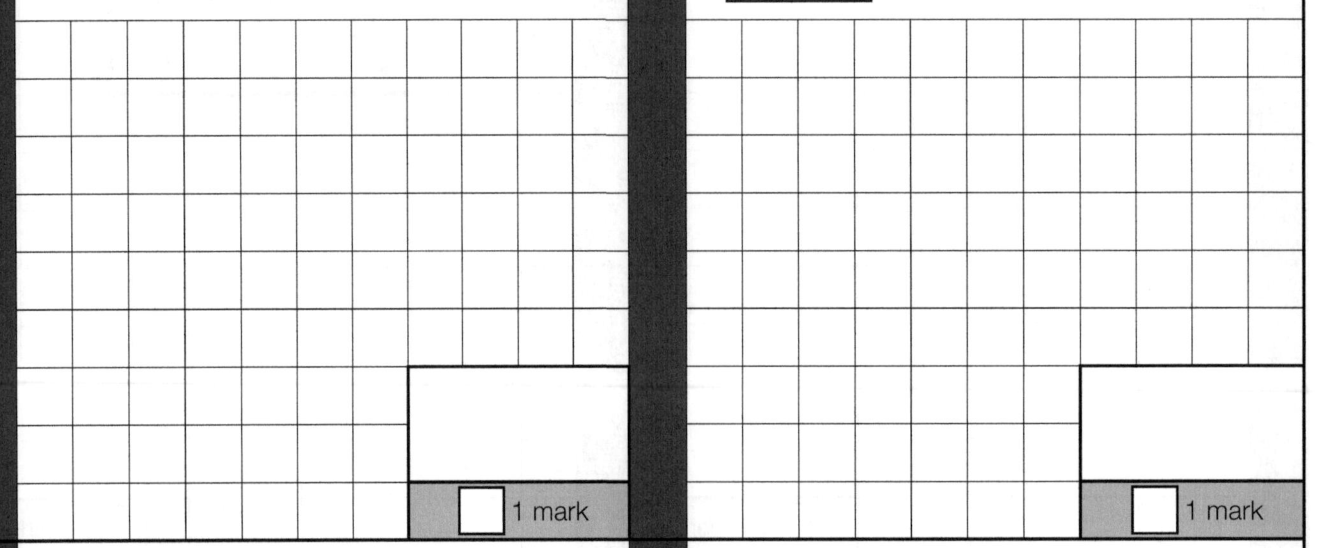

1 mark

1 mark

5 $48 \times 1\frac{1}{4} =$

6 $76 + (72 \div 9) =$

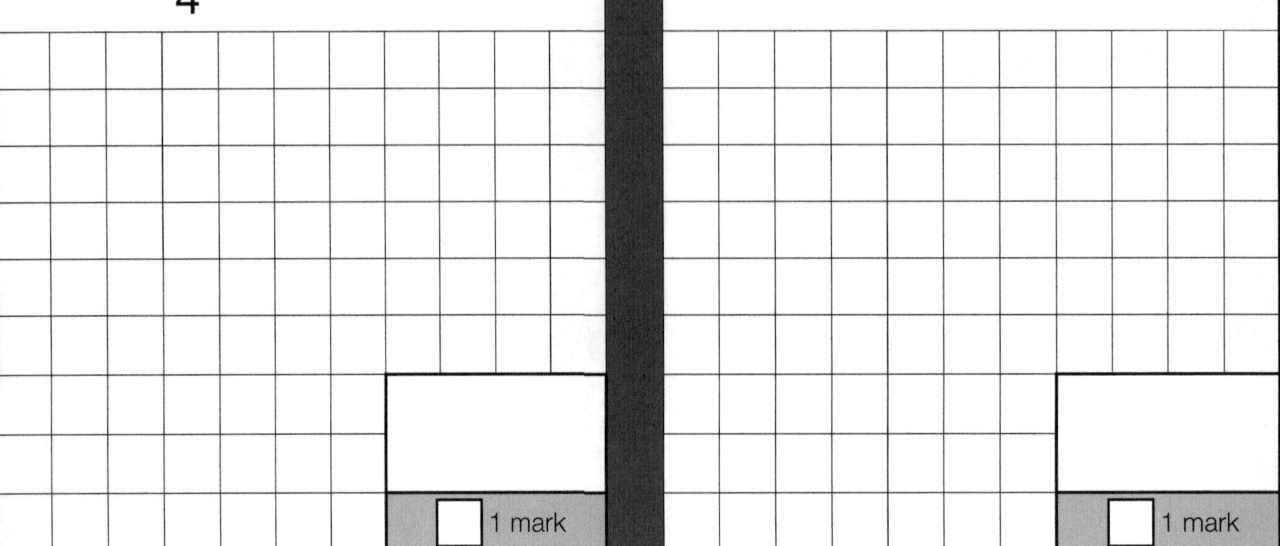

1 mark

1 mark

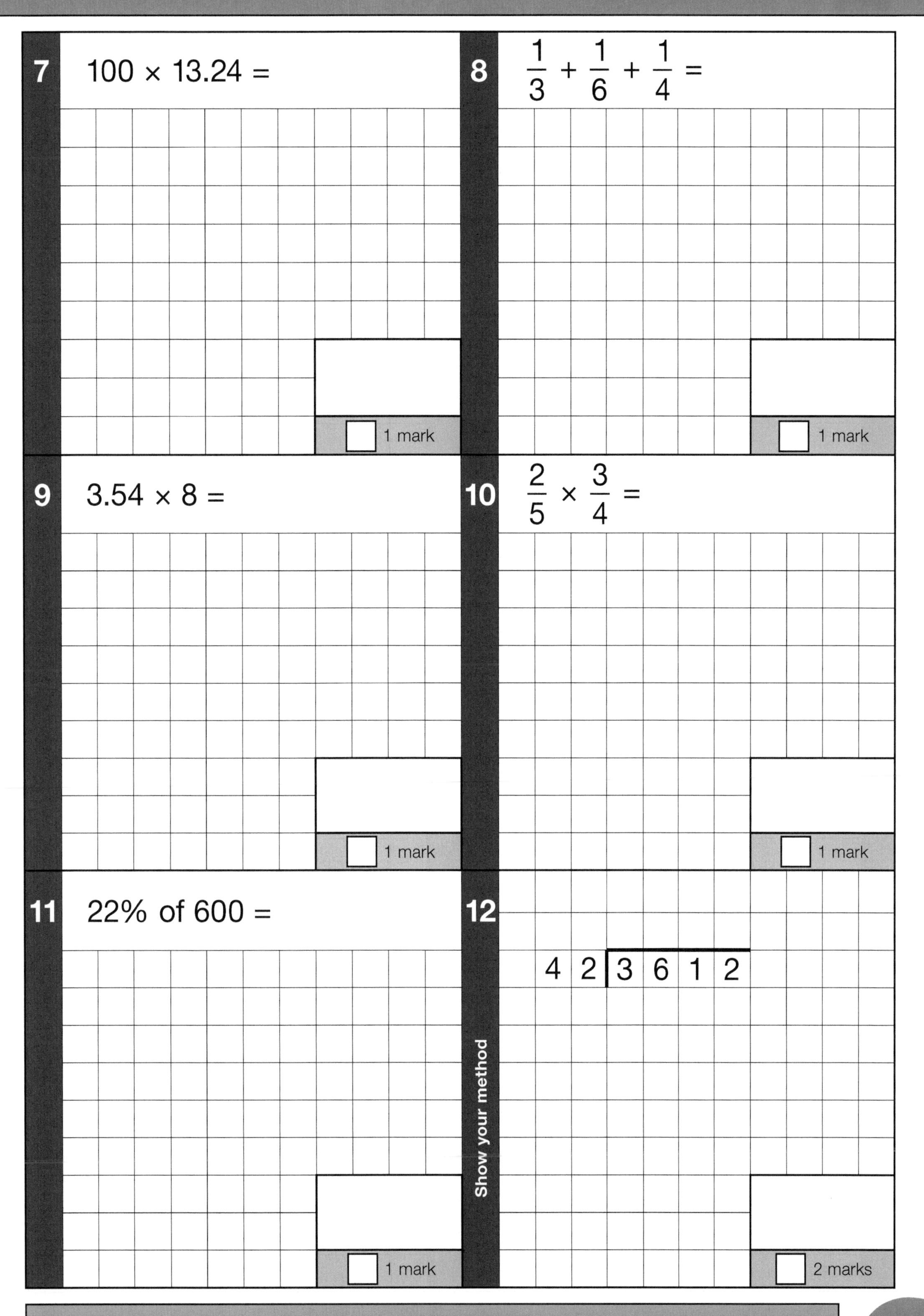

7 $100 \times 13.24 =$

1 mark

8 $\frac{1}{3} + \frac{1}{6} + \frac{1}{4} =$

1 mark

9 $3.54 \times 8 =$

1 mark

10 $\frac{2}{5} \times \frac{3}{4} =$

1 mark

11 22% of 600 =

1 mark

12 $42 \overline{)3612}$

Show your method

2 marks

Test 3 total marks ..../13

Arithmetic Test 4

10 min

1 1,000 + 220 = ☐

1 mark

2 $\frac{7}{8} - \frac{3}{8} =$

1 mark

3 5,361 − 1,424 =

1 mark

4 108 ÷ 12 =

1 mark

5 $5^2 + 3^3 =$

1 mark

6 $\frac{1}{2} \div 2 =$

1 mark

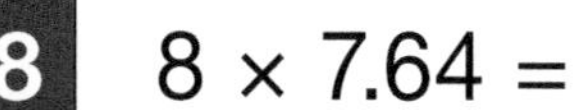

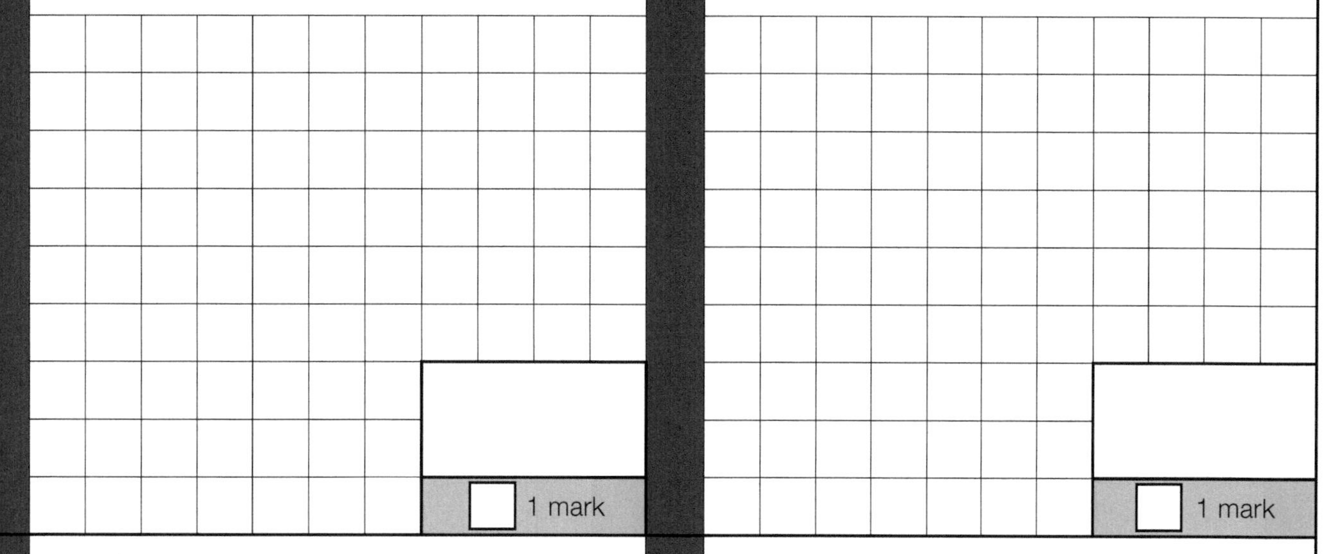

7 15% of 800 =

1 mark

8 $8 \times 7.64 =$

1 mark

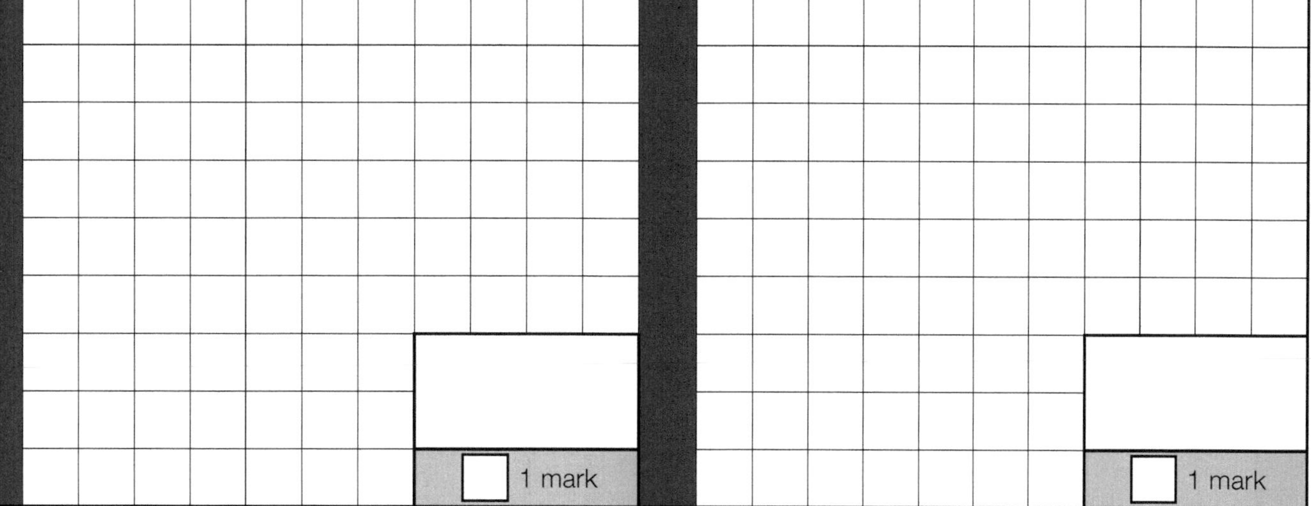

9 $2\frac{1}{2} \times 18 =$

1 mark

10 $42.42 \times 10 =$

1 mark

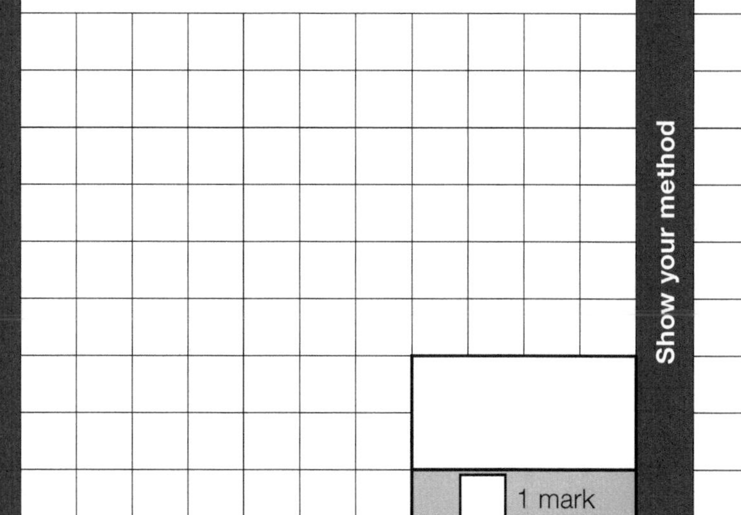

11 $2\frac{1}{3} + 1\frac{3}{4} =$

1 mark

12

$27 \overline{)364}$

Show your method

2 marks

Test 4 total marks ..../13

Arithmetic Test 5

10 min

1 $46 + 225 =$

1 mark

2 $4 \times 0 \times 1 =$

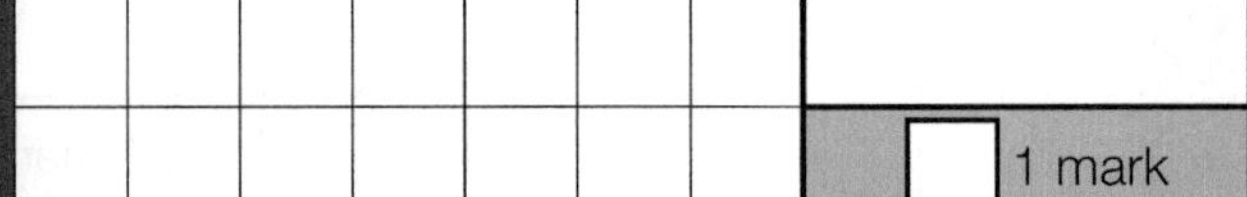

1 mark

3 $\square \times 11 = 132$

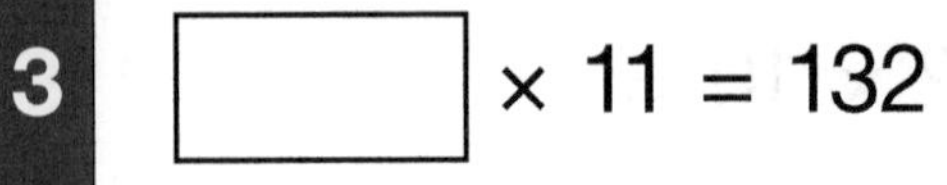

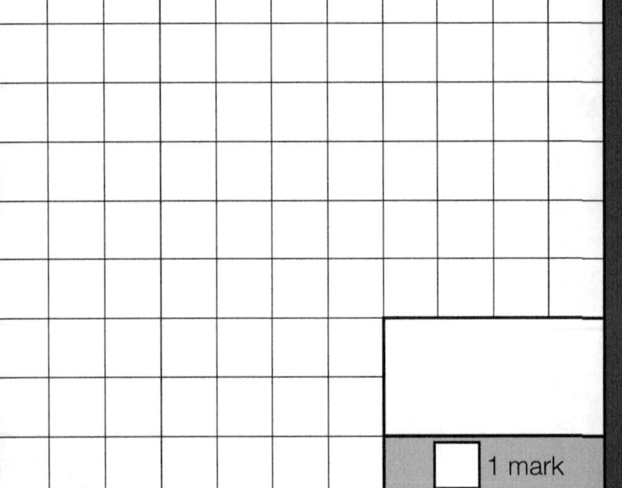

1 mark

4

$$\begin{array}{r} 402 \\ \times \quad 19 \\ \hline \end{array}$$

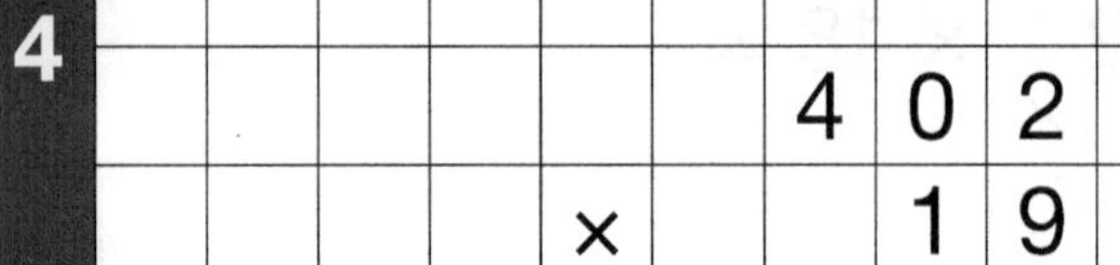

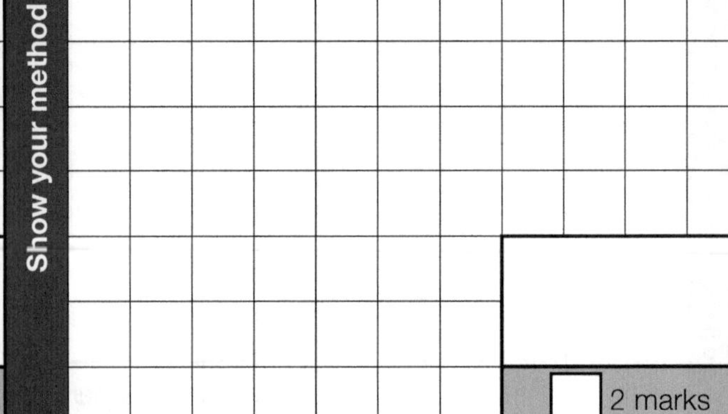

Show your method

2 marks

5 $88 \times 2\frac{1}{2} =$

1 mark

6 $42 \div (7 \times 6) =$

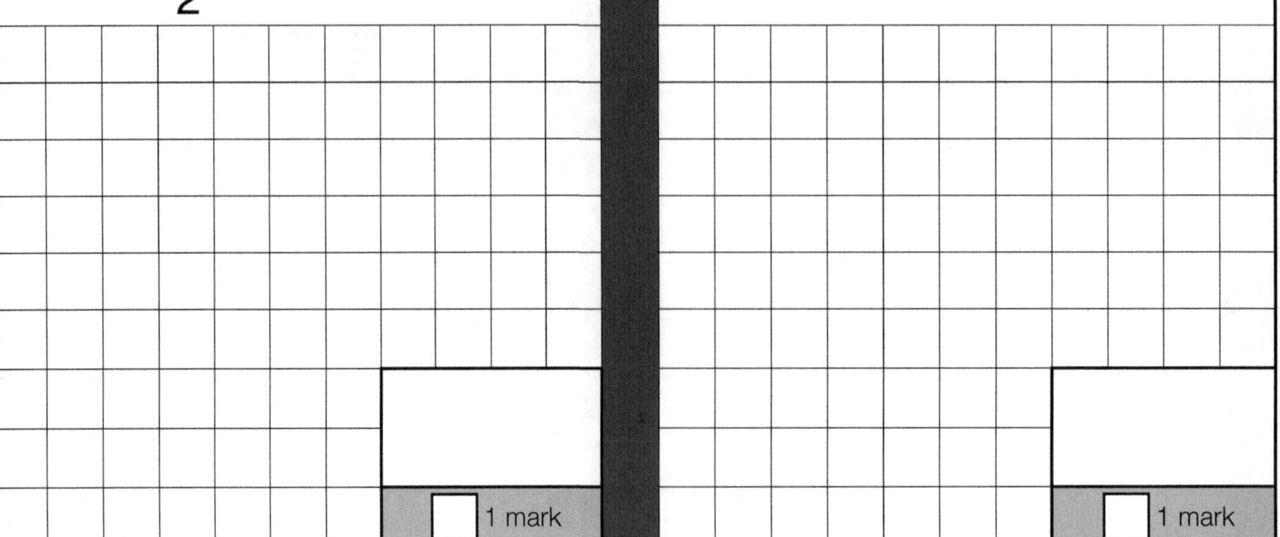

1 mark

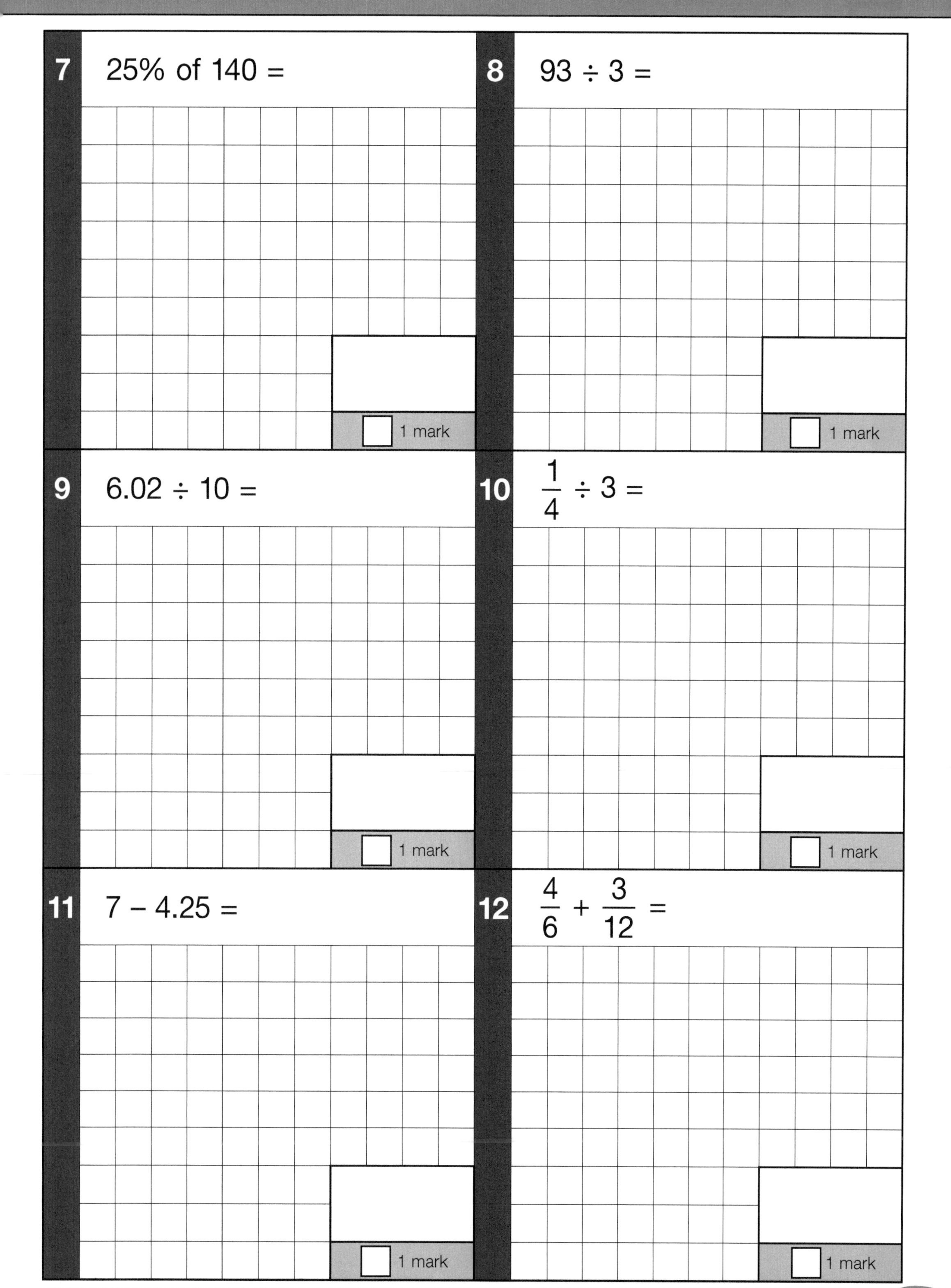

7 25% of 140 =

1 mark

8 93 ÷ 3 =

1 mark

9 6.02 ÷ 10 =

1 mark

10 $\frac{1}{4} \div 3 =$

1 mark

11 7 – 4.25 =

1 mark

12 $\frac{4}{6} + \frac{3}{12} =$

1 mark

Test 5 total marks ..../13

Arithmetic Test 6

10 min

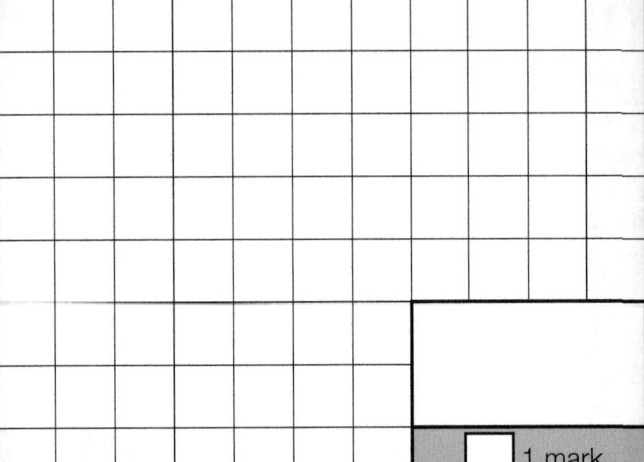

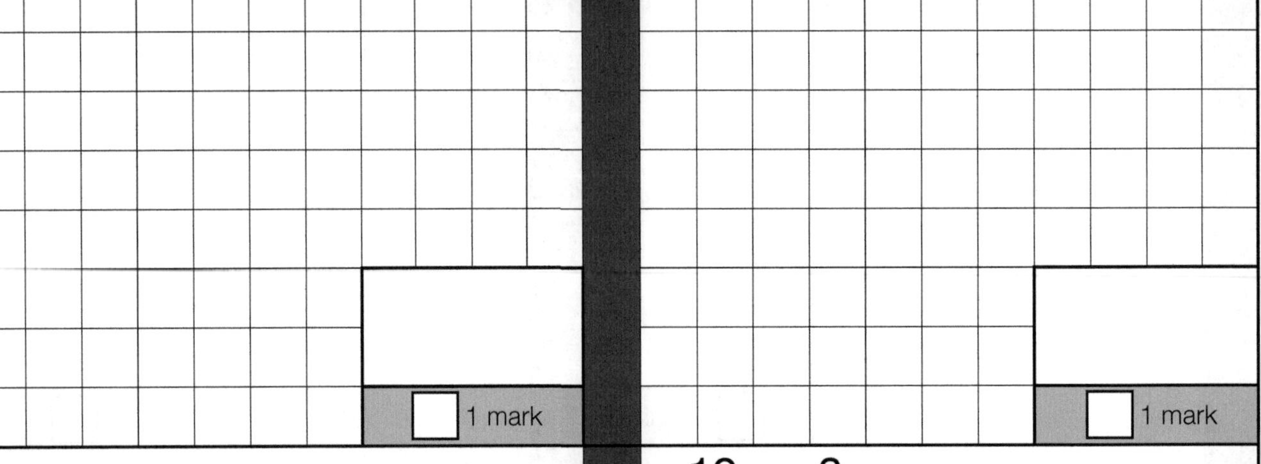

1 $\square + 100 = 222$

1 mark

2 $49 \div \square = 7$

1 mark

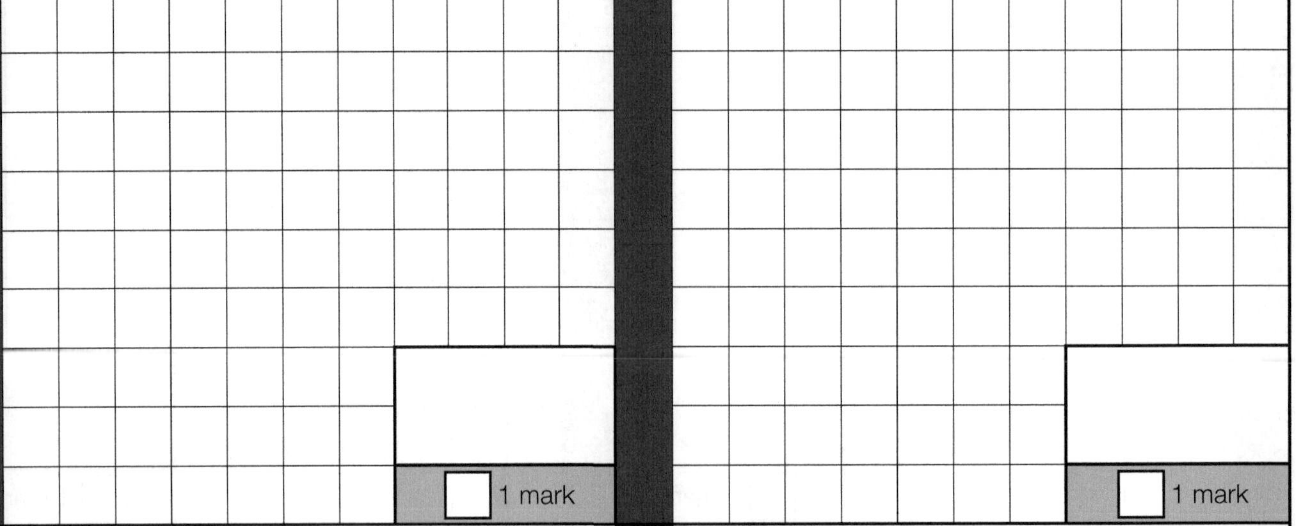

3 $464 + \square = 574$

1 mark

4 $\frac{12}{18} - \frac{3}{18} =$

1 mark

5 $\frac{10}{15} - \frac{1}{3} =$

1 mark

6 $3.62 + 2.05 =$

1 mark

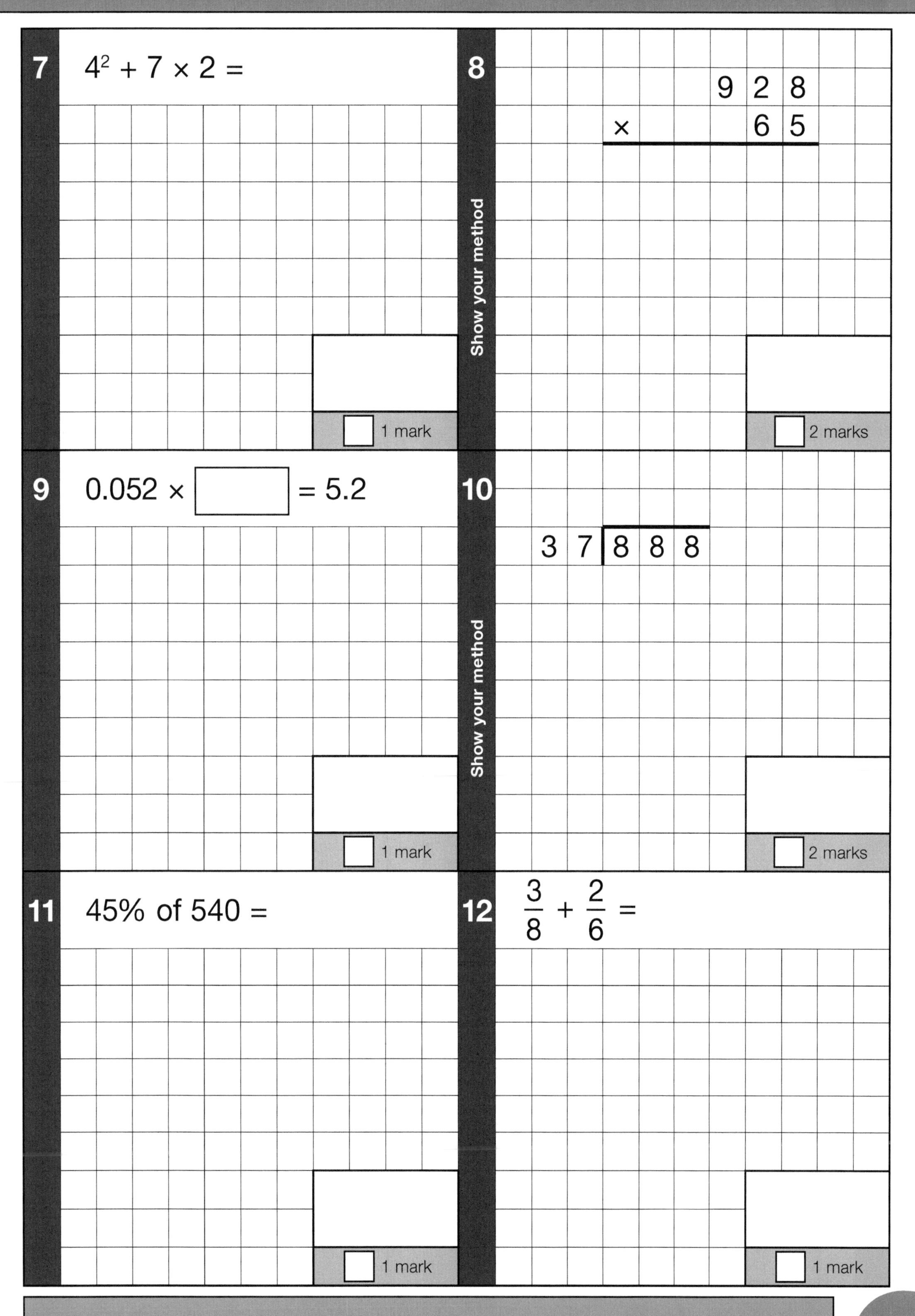

7 $4^2 + 7 \times 2 =$

1 mark

8

$$\begin{array}{r} 928 \\ \times \quad 65 \\ \hline \end{array}$$

Show your method

2 marks

9 $0.052 \times \square = 5.2$

1 mark

10

$37\overline{)888}$

Show your method

2 marks

11 45% of 540 =

1 mark

12 $\frac{3}{8} + \frac{2}{6} =$

1 mark

Test 6 total marks ..../14

10 min

Arithmetic Test 7

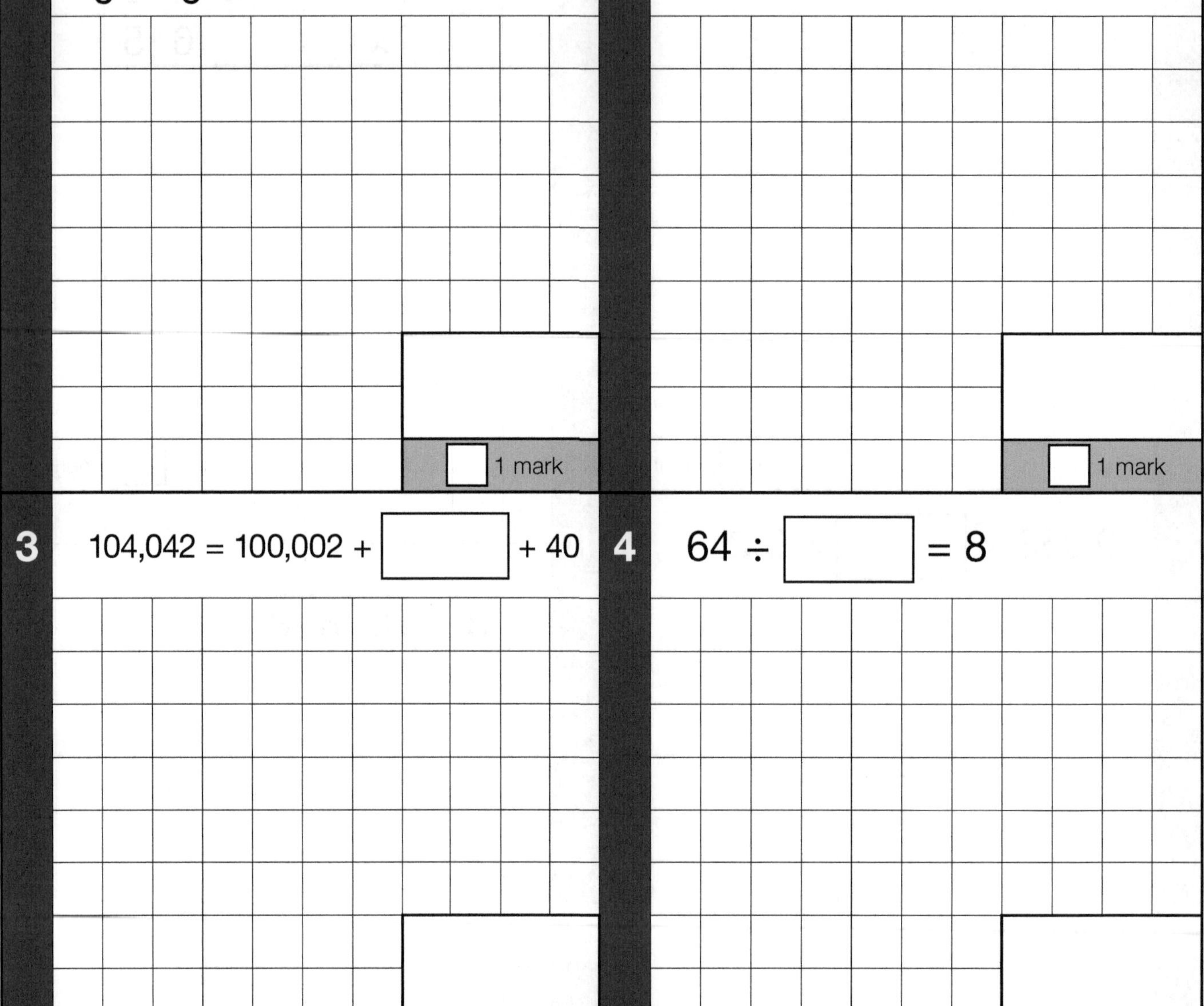

1 $\frac{2}{9} + \frac{6}{9} =$

1 mark

2 $46 \times 7 =$

1 mark

3 104,042 = 100,002 + ☐ + 40

1 mark

4 64 ÷ ☐ = 8

1 mark

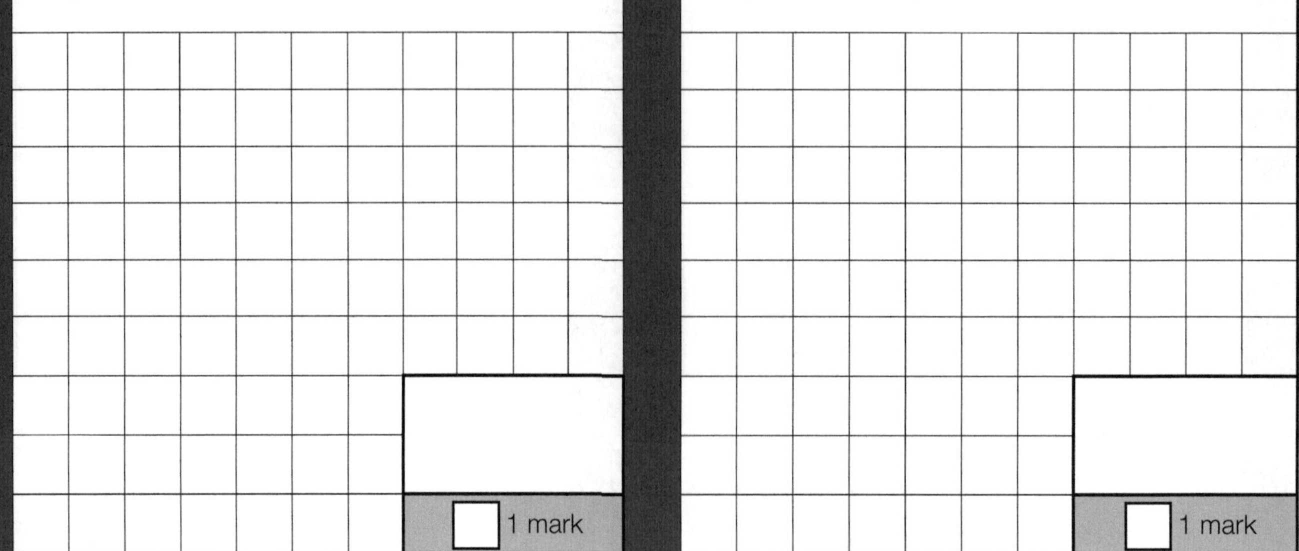

5 7,615 – 231 =

1 mark

6 3,641 ÷ 1,000 =

1 mark

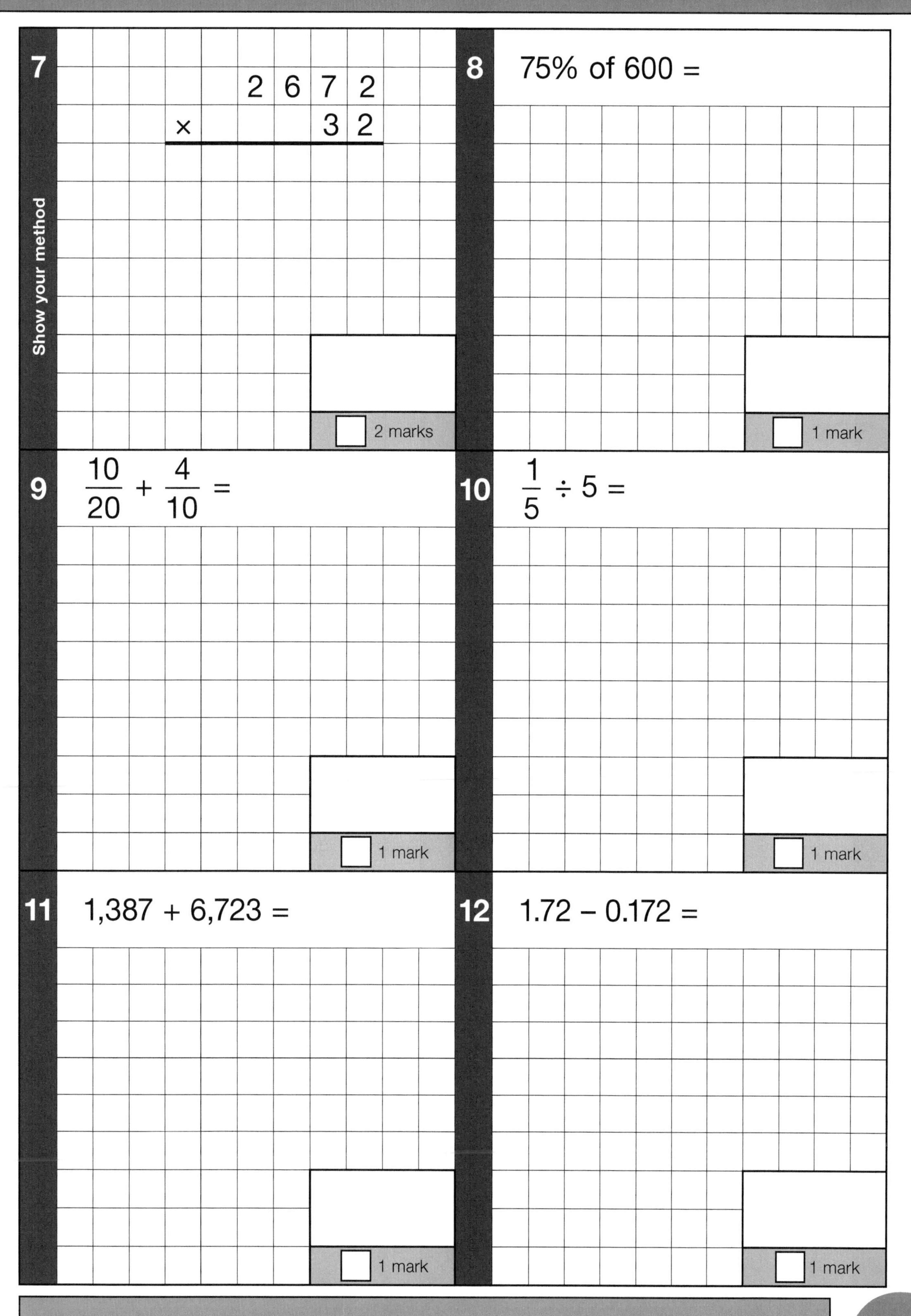

7

$$\begin{array}{r} 2672 \\ \times \quad 32 \\ \hline \end{array}$$

Show your method

2 marks

8 75% of 600 =

1 mark

9 $\frac{10}{20} + \frac{4}{10} =$

1 mark

10 $\frac{1}{5} \div 5 =$

1 mark

11 1,387 + 6,723 =

1 mark

12 1.72 − 0.172 =

1 mark

Test 7 total marks ..../13

Arithmetic Test 8

10 min

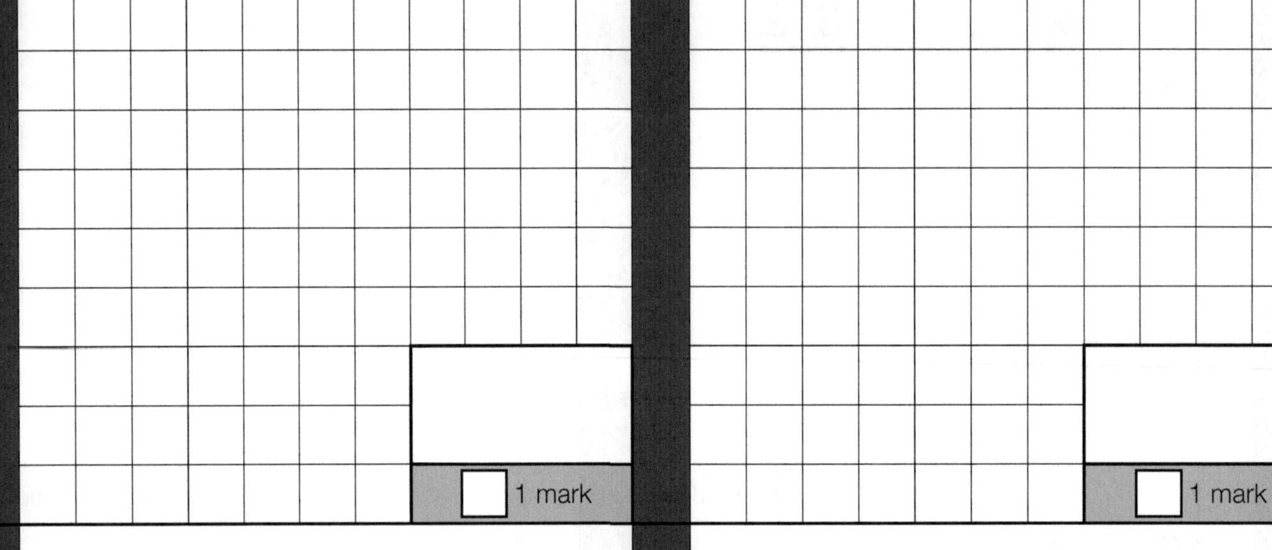

1 $8 \times 25 =$

1 mark

2 $420 \div 6 =$

1 mark

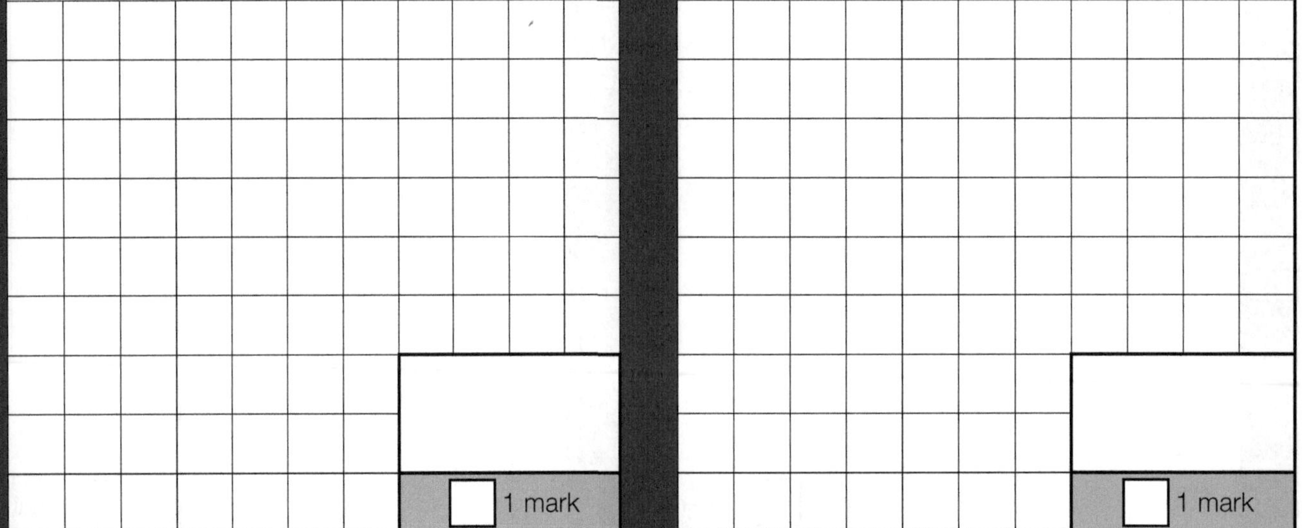

3 $6 - 2.65 =$

1 mark

4 $4.5 + 5.132 =$

1 mark

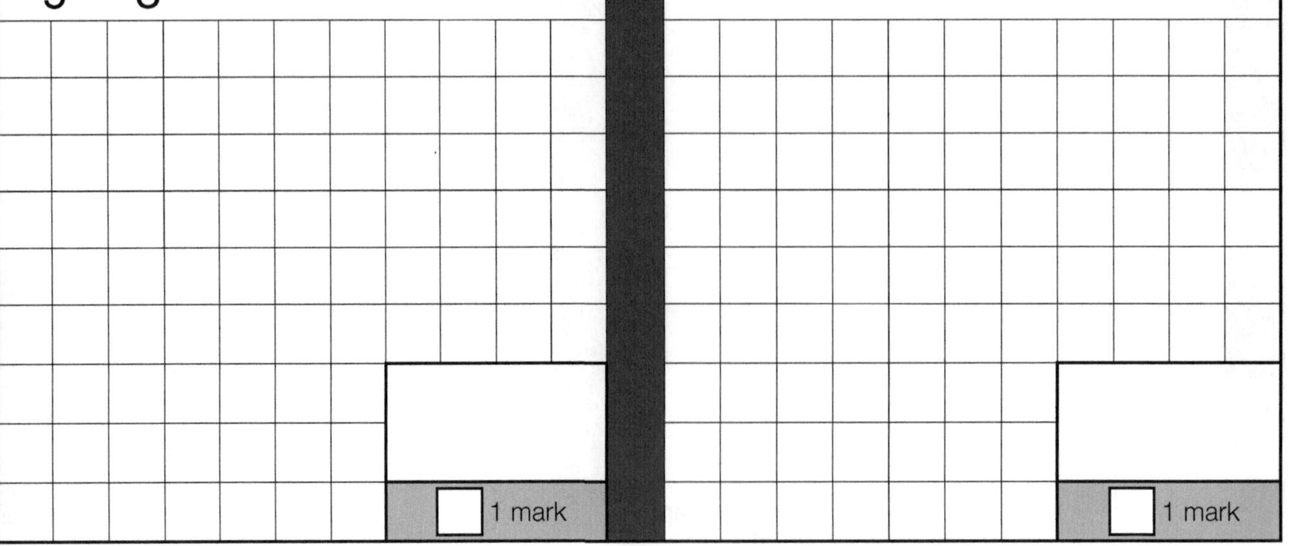

5 $\frac{3}{9} - \frac{1}{3} =$

1 mark

6 $80 \times 70 =$

1 mark

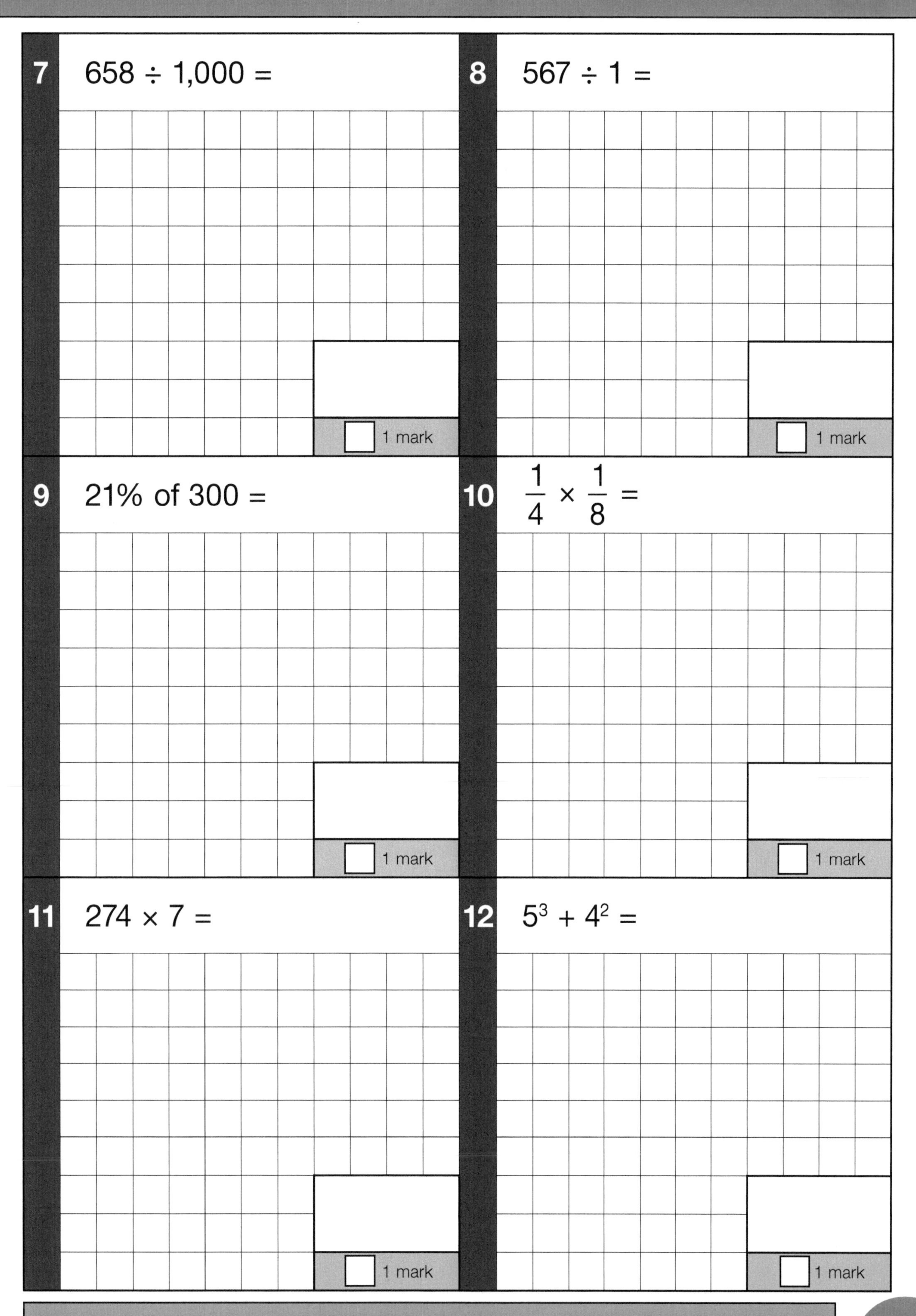

7 $658 \div 1{,}000 =$

1 mark

8 $567 \div 1 =$

1 mark

9 21% of $300 =$

1 mark

10 $\frac{1}{4} \times \frac{1}{8} =$

1 mark

11 $274 \times 7 =$

1 mark

12 $5^3 + 4^2 =$

1 mark

Test 8 total marks ..../12

Reasoning Test 1

1 Josie uses a mental method to calculate 263 – 76. She starts from 263

Here are some methods that Josie could use.

Tick the methods that are **correct**.

Subtract 200 and add 63 ☐

Add 13 then subtract 76 ☐

Subtract 63 then subtract 13 ☐

Subtract 6 then subtract 70 ☐

2 marks

2 Tick the two numbers that are equivalent to $\frac{3}{4}$

Tick **two**.

$\frac{75}{100}$	☐	$\frac{3}{10}$	☐
$\frac{1}{2}$	☐	0.75	☐

1 mark

3 Scott and Bella make a scale model of their house. Their house is 10 metres wide and 8 metres tall.

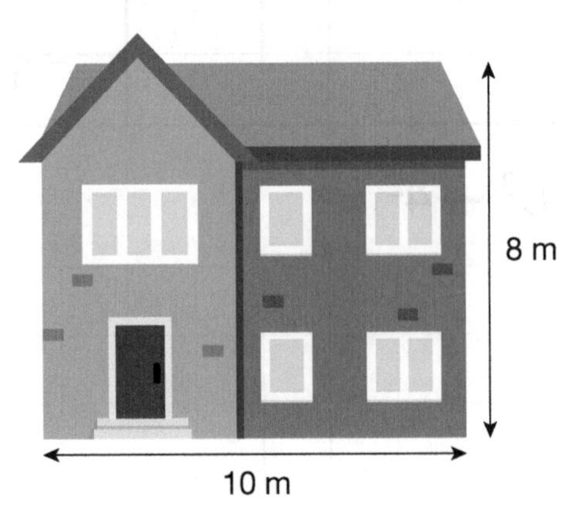

Their model is 20 cm wide.

How tall is their model house?

☐ cm

1 mark

4 The children in Year 6 carried out a survey to find out how many Key Stage 1 and Key Stage 2 pupils eat fruit every day.

The graph shows the results.

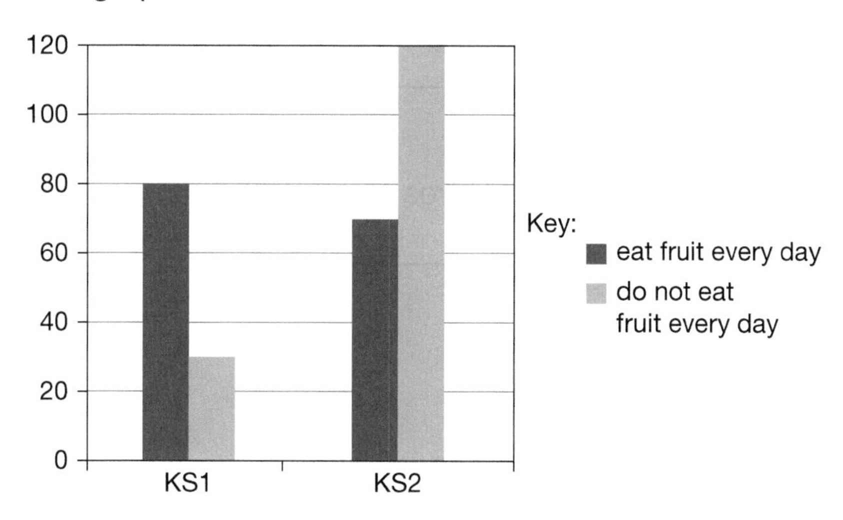

a) How many children in total eat fruit every day?

1 mark

b) How many more Key Stage 2 children than Key Stage 1 children do not eat fruit every day?

1 mark

5 Ravi takes a ride on a Ferris wheel.

The Ferris wheel goes around twice.

How many degrees does the Ferris wheel turn through?

1 mark

6 The numbers in this sequence decrease by the same amount each time.

Write the missing numbers.

81 ☐ 63 54 ☐ ☐

2 marks

7 Mark a point on the line that is 5.6 centimetres from point A.

A

1 mark

8 The Year 5 pupils are selling pizza at the school fair.

A plain pizza costs £2

They use the formula below to work out the price of a pizza:

price of a pizza = £2 + number of toppings × 30p

a) How much will Tommy pay for a pizza with 4 toppings?

☐

1 mark

b) Sabrina has £4. What is the greatest number of toppings she could have on a pizza?

Show your method

☐ toppings

2 marks

Total marks .... /13

Reasoning Test 2

1 Write these numbers in size order, starting with the smallest.

1.004 0.4 0.423 0.43

☐ ☐ ☐ ☐

1 mark

2 Amy completes this addition calculation.

	4	3
+	3	2
	7	5

Write a subtraction calculation she could use to check her answer.

	☐	☐
–	☐	☐
	☐	☐

1 mark

3 Mr Hasid tells the class that he is thinking of a number.

He multiplies his number by 3

He rounds this number to the nearest 10

He now has 40

Write all of the possible numbers Mr Hasid could have started with.

....

2 marks

4 An explorer has found two dinosaur bones.

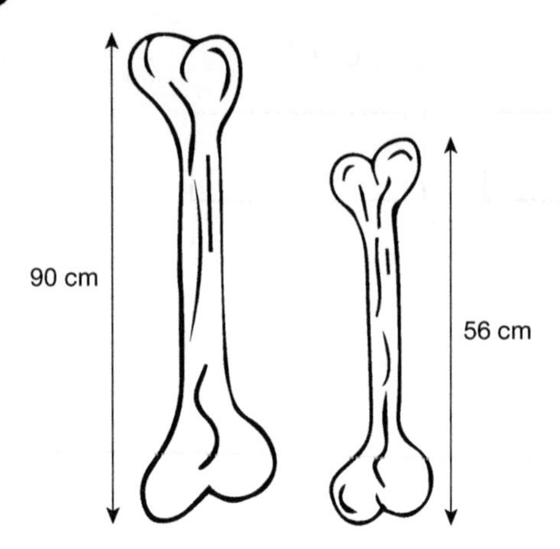

To estimate the total length of each dinosaur, the explorer multiplies the length of each bone by 8.

What is the difference in the estimated length of the two dinosaurs?

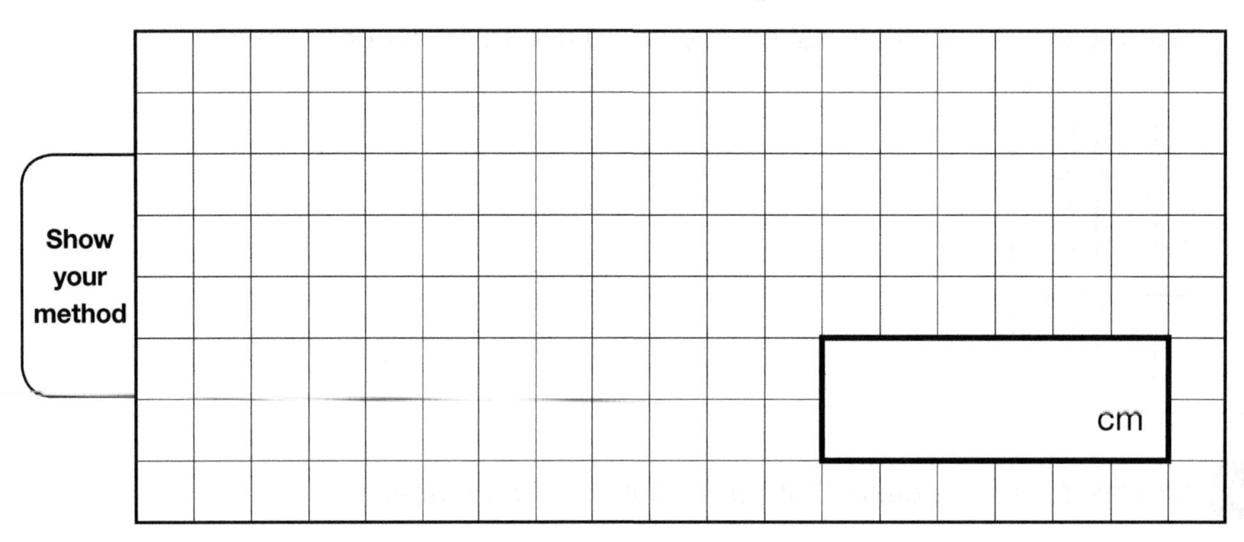

2 marks

5 The face of a cube has an area of 9 cm^2

What is the volume of the cube?

☐ cm^3

1 mark

6 The vertices of a triangle have these coordinates:

(–4, –2) (2, 5) (3, –3)

Draw the triangle on the grid.

One vertex has been plotted for you.

y
5
4
3
2
1
–5 –4 –3 –2 –1 0 1 2 3 4 5 x
–1
–2
–3
–4
–5
(3, –3)

1 mark

7 Write the five factors of 48 that are not multiples of 3 or 12.

☐ ☐ ☐ ☐ ☐

2 marks

8 29 children are sewing a banner.

Their teacher has 11.5 metres of thread.

Each child is given 350 mm of thread.

How much thread is left over?

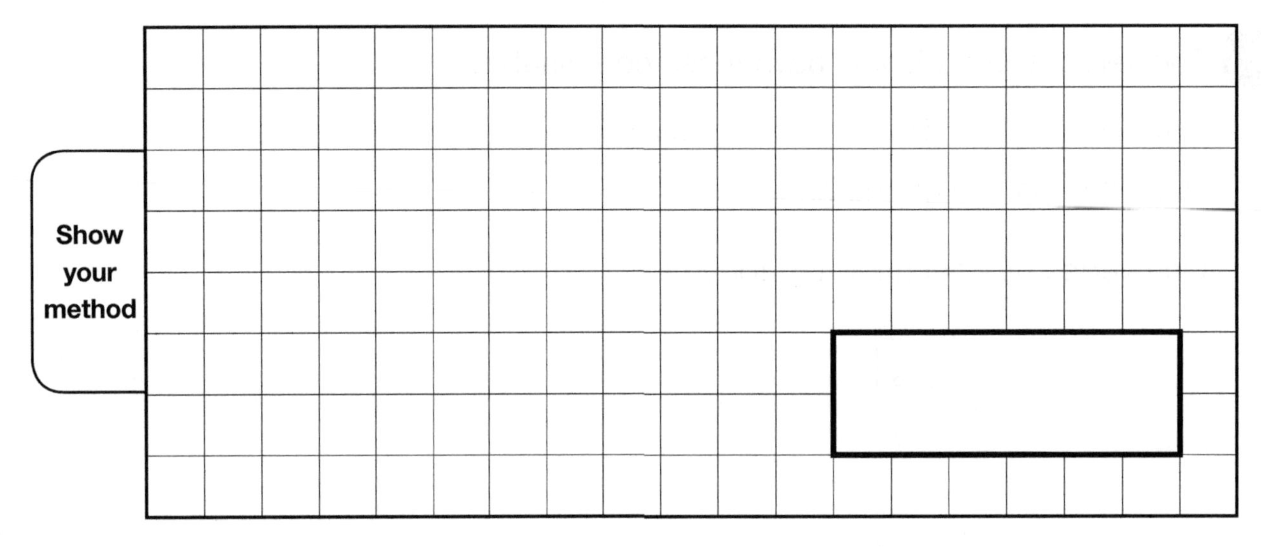

3 marks

9 Look at this pattern of number pairs.

a	*b*
12	3
15	4
18	5
21	6

Complete the rule for this pattern.

$a = b \times \square + 3$

1 mark

Reasoning Test 3

1 What is the next number in this sequence?

203,040 204,040 205,040 206,040 ☐

1 mark

2 Tick the shape below that has both parallel and perpendicular lines.

1 mark

3 Write the missing numbers.

2 years = ☐ months

56 days = ☐ weeks

600 minutes = ☐ hours

2 marks

4 Circle the fraction that is equivalent to $9\frac{2}{3}$

$\frac{19}{6}$ $\frac{18}{3}$ $\frac{29}{3}$ $\frac{27}{3}$

1 mark

5 Finley's book shows the year it was published in Roman numerals.

MMXVI

Write the year MMXVI in figures.

☐

1 mark

6 The graph shows the monthly average temperatures for a village.

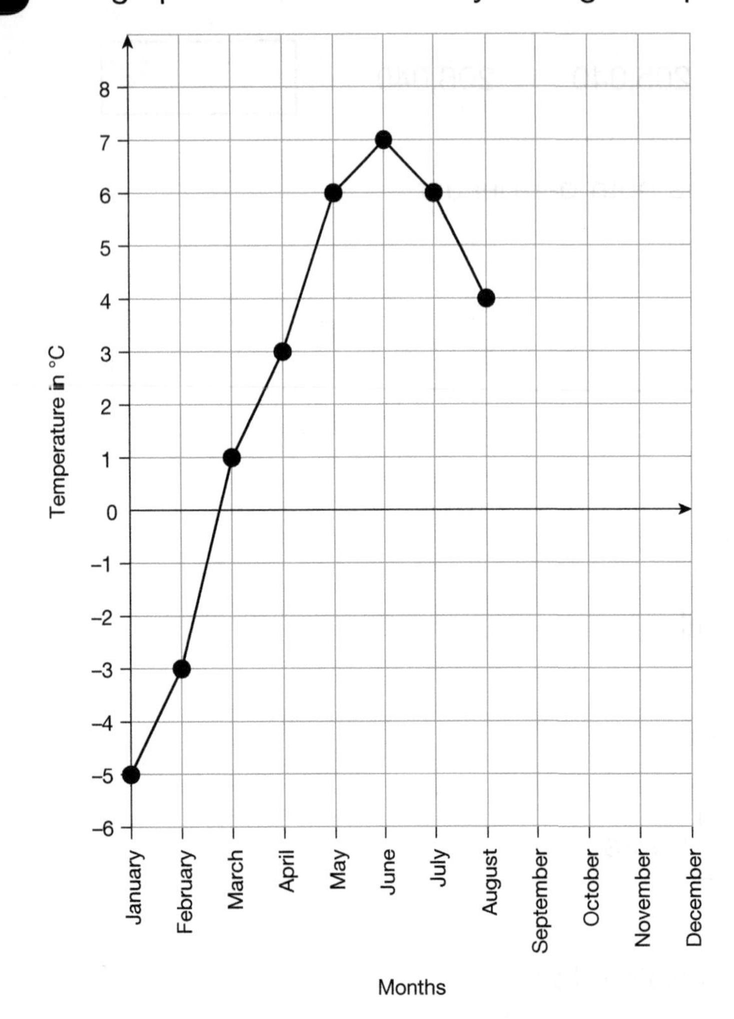

a) How many degrees colder is the average January temperature than the average July temperature?

☐ °C

1 mark

b) The August average temperature is 8°C higher than the December average. Work out the average temperature for December.

☐ °C

1 mark

7 Complete the sequence by writing the missing numbers.

$1\frac{1}{2}$ $1\frac{3}{4}$ ☐ $2\frac{1}{4}$ ☐ $2\frac{3}{4}$

2 marks

8 The shape on the grid has been translated from its original position.

In its original position, A was at (2, 9).

Draw the shape in its original position. Use a ruler.

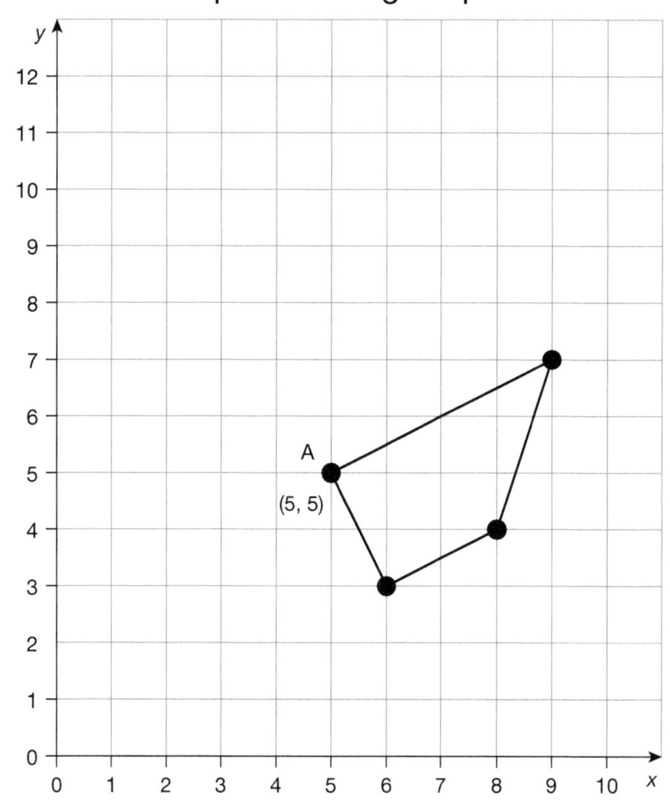

1 mark

9 Casey buys a multipack of 9 yoghurts for £5.99

Mari buys 9 individual yoghurts for 82p each.

How much more does Mari pay than Casey?

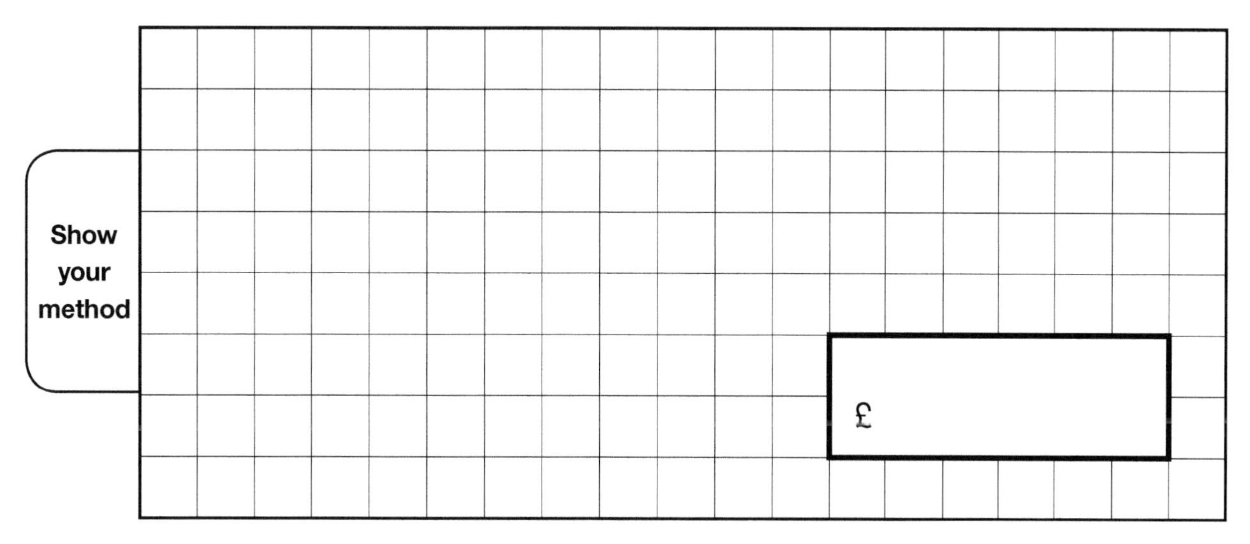

2 marks

Reasoning Test 4

1 Class 6b has three packs of 36 large exercise books and 4 packs of 18 small exercise books.

How many exercise books does the class have altogether?

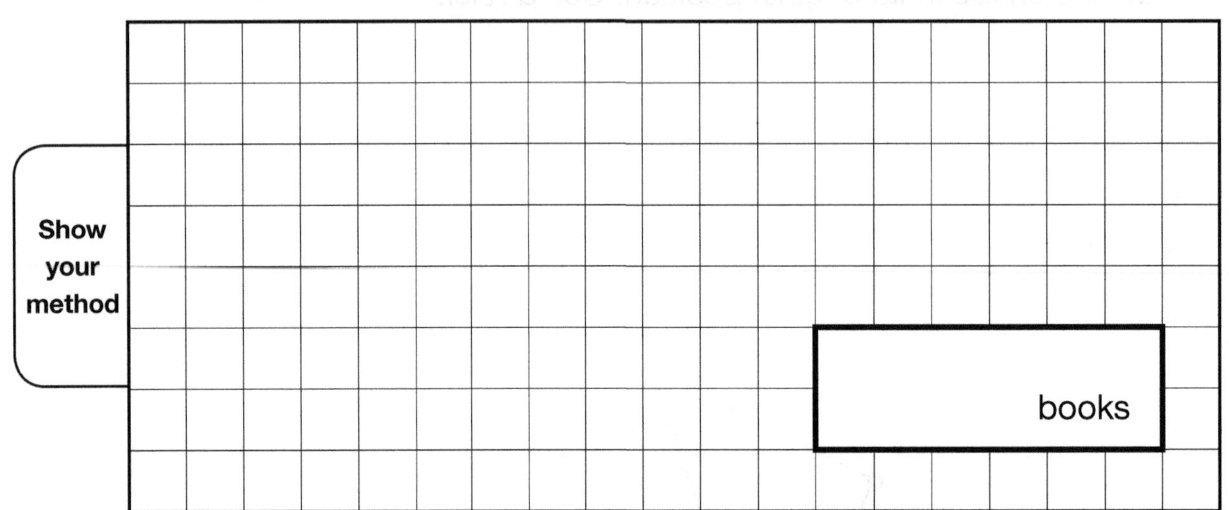

2 marks

2 Here is a shape on a grid.

Complete the shape so that it is symmetrical about the mirror line.

Use a ruler.

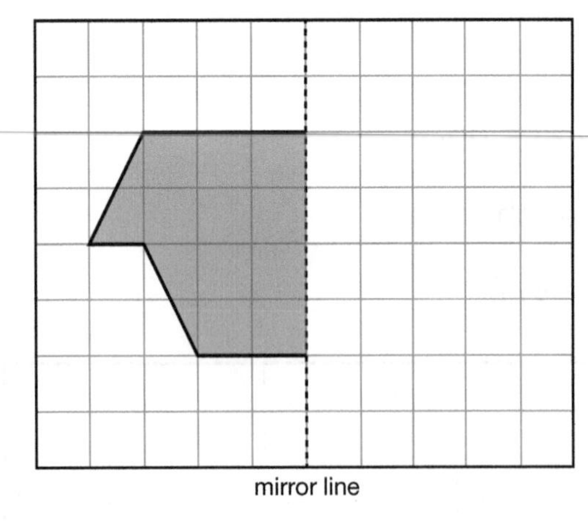

1 mark

3 Write these fractions in order in the boxes below, starting with the smallest.

$\frac{4}{3}$ $\frac{6}{5}$ $\frac{5}{4}$

 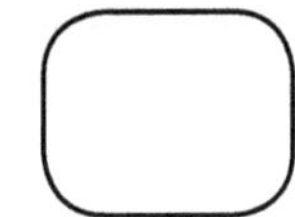 

1 mark

4 Elan has four number cards.

She uses each card once to make a four-digit number. She places:

- 3 in the hundreds column
- 2 so that it has a higher value than any of the other digits
- the remaining two digits so that the four-digit number is a multiple of 5

Write a digit in each box to show Elan's four-digit number.

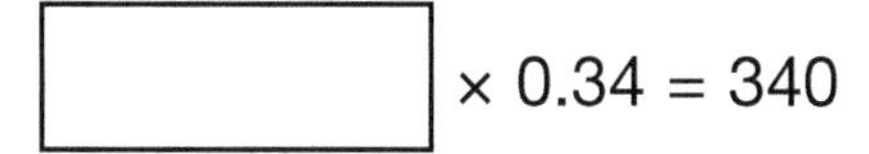

1 mark

5 Write the missing number to make this multiplication correct.

$\square \times 0.34 = 340$

1 mark

6 Amy says,

I had 12 football stickers.
I gave some to my friend.

Which expression below shows the amount of stickers that Amy has left?

a is the amount of stickers Amy gave away.

Tick **one**.

$12 \times a$	☐	$a + 12$	☐
$12 - a$	☐	$a - 12$	☐

1 mark

7 The chart below shows where children in Year 6 at Park View School went on holiday.

All 28 children in the class went on holiday.

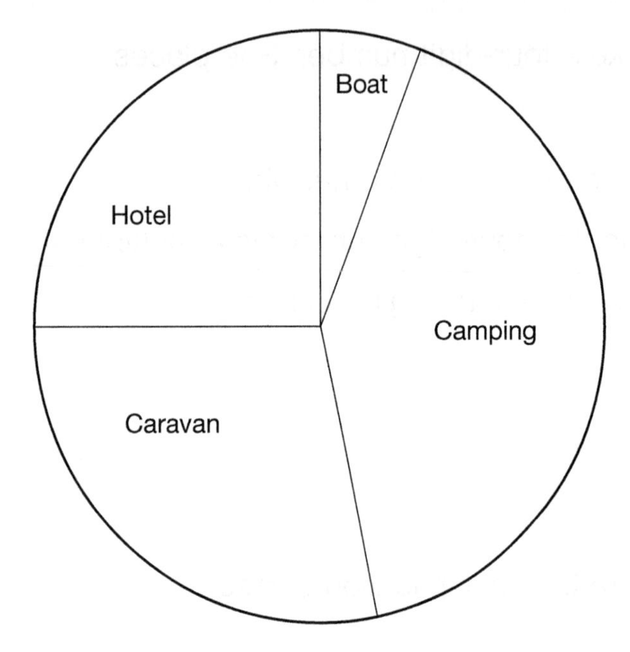

Look at the statements about the chart.

Tick the statements that are true.

7 children stayed in a hotel.	☐
Less than 50% of the children went camping.	☐
More than 14 children stayed in a caravan.	☐
More than 7 children stayed on a boat.	☐

2 marks

8 On Friday, 1,624 guests were staying in Green Valley Holiday Park.

On Saturday:

- 789 more guests arrived
- 568 guests left.

How many guests were in Green Valley Holiday Park at the end of Saturday?

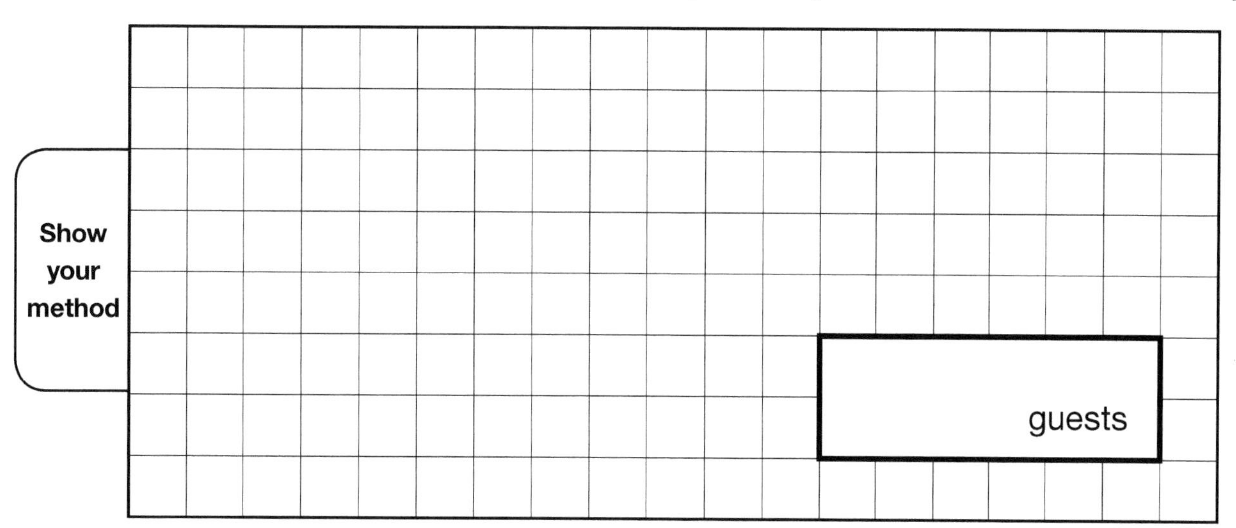

2 marks

9 The total value of the numbers in each row of the table below is equal.

Missing numbers are represented by x. Every x in the table has the same value.

23	0	1	2	x
x	22	0	0	x
12	x	x	x	6

Work out the value of x.

x =

1 mark

10 min

Reasoning Test 5

1 Tick the shapes that have $\frac{2}{3}$ shaded.

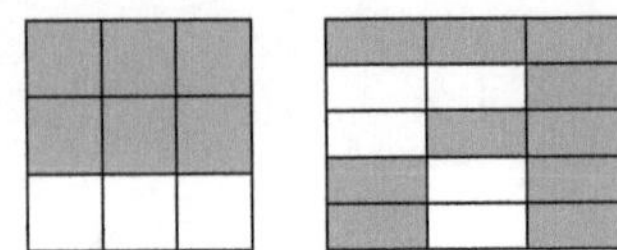
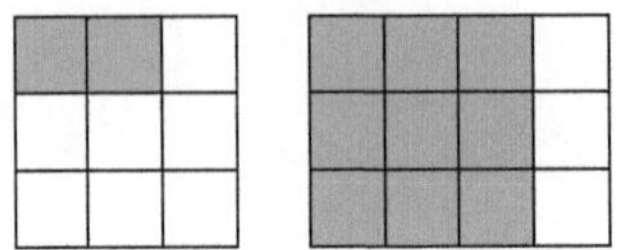

1 mark

2 Tick the 3-D shape that has the same number of vertices as faces.

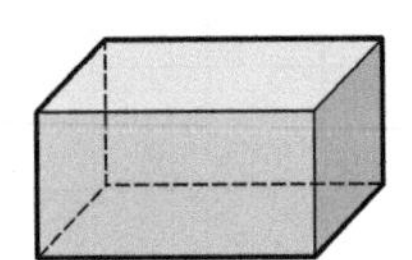
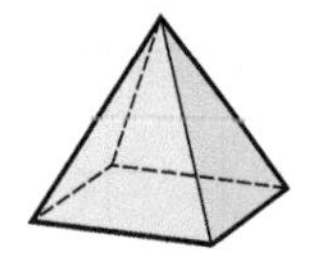
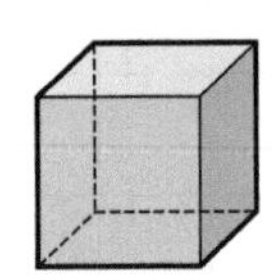
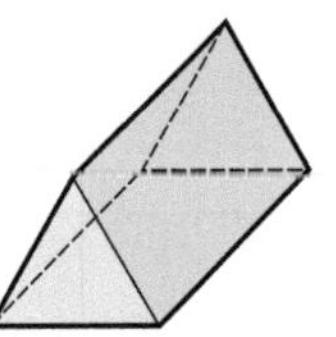

1 mark

3 Eliyan receives £5 pocket money per week.

He saves £1 of his pocket money each week.

This means he saves  % of his pocket money per week.

1 mark

4 3,200 plastic bottles are collected from local beaches.

750 are collected from Sandy Cove.

1,400 are collected from South Shore.

The rest are collected from North Sands and Hope Cove. Equal numbers are collected from each of these two beaches.

How many plastic bottles are collected from North Sands?

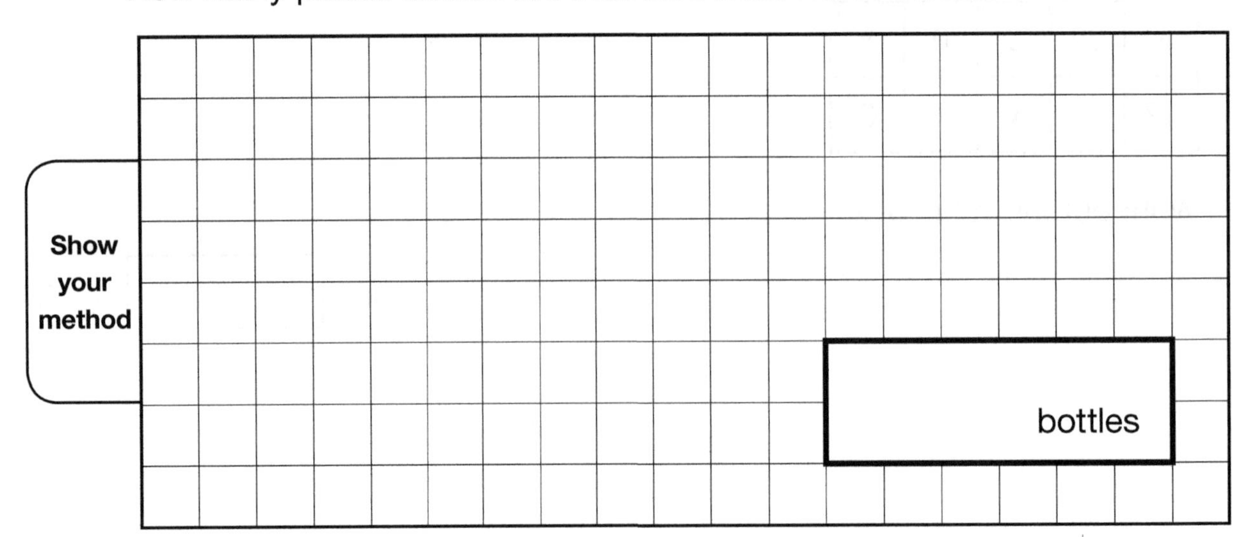

2 marks

5 Amy recorded the temperature in different places around her house at 7am and 7pm one winter day.

Place	Temperature	
	7am	7pm
Kitchen	14°C	20°C
Shed	–1°C	3°C
Cellar	6°C	6°C
Yard	–5°C	1°C

a) At 7am, how many degrees warmer was the kitchen than the yard?

[ ] degrees

1 mark

b) Which place was 4 degrees colder in the morning than in the evening?

[ ]

1 mark

6 These cuboids have the same volume.

Cuboid A

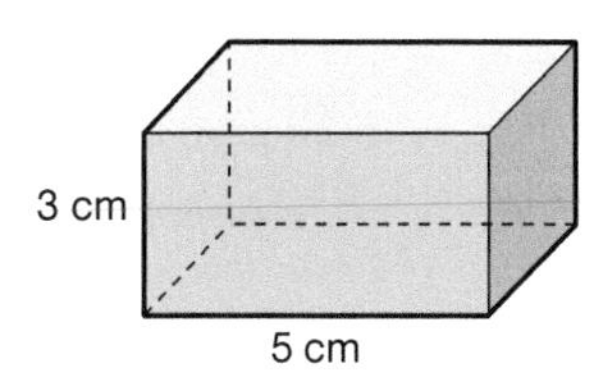

Cuboid B

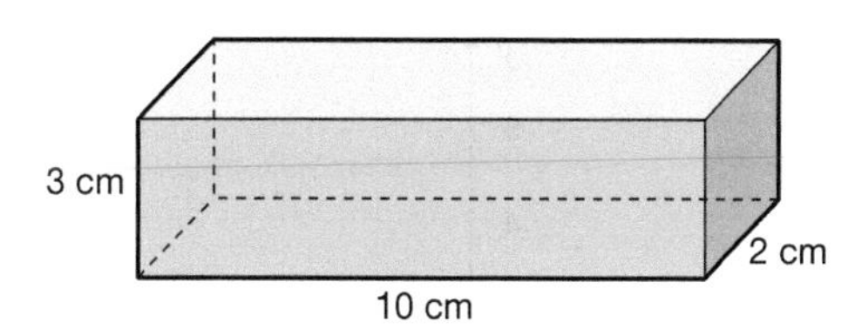

Calculate the missing length for cuboid A.

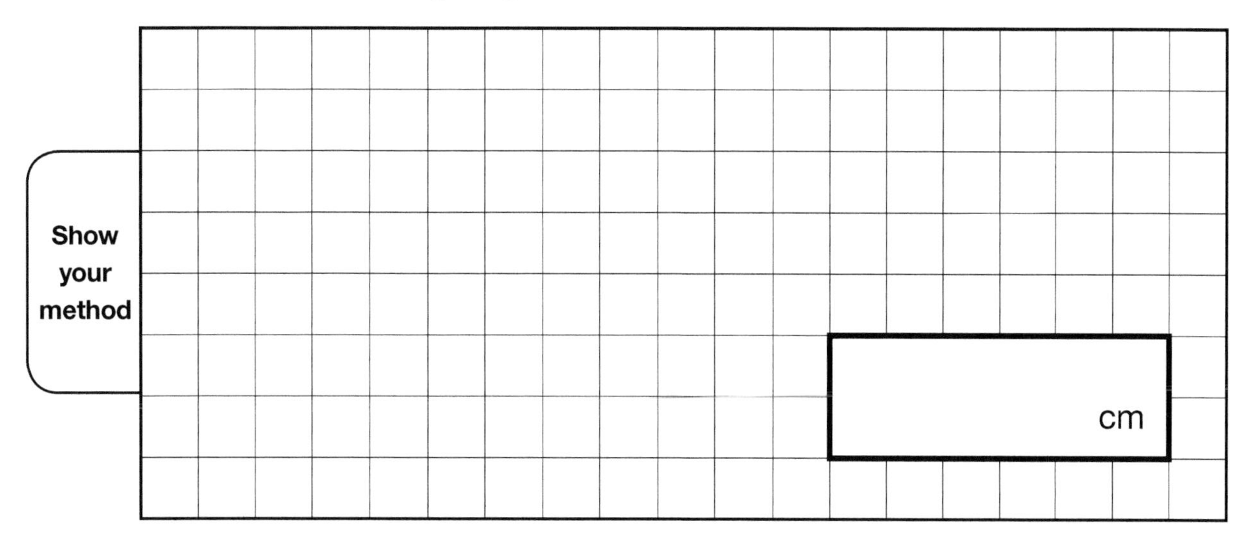

2 marks

7 Ademola says,

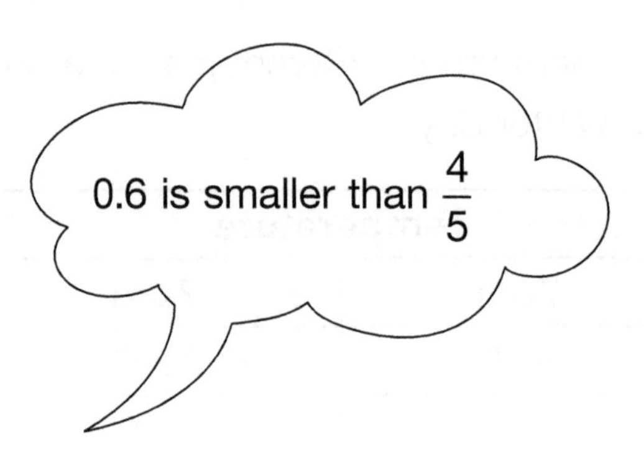

Explain why he is correct.

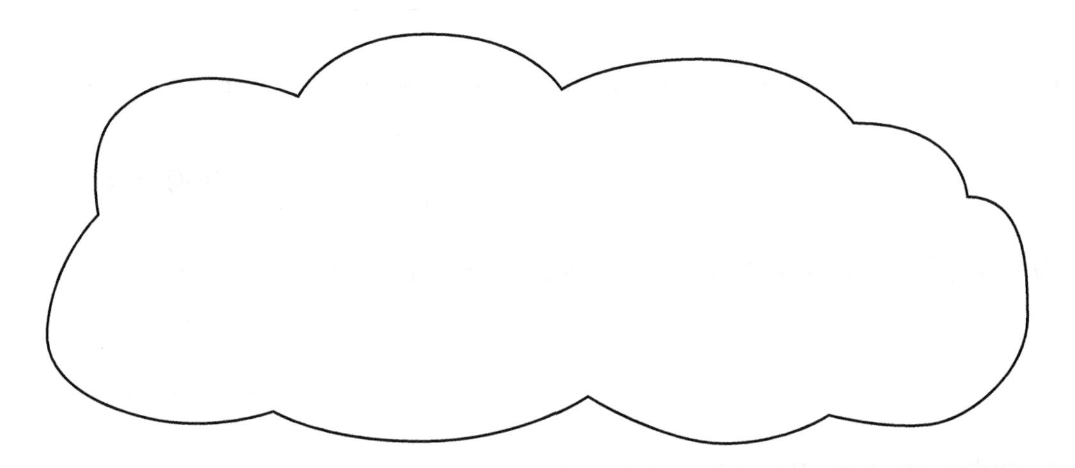

1 mark

8 Tamara draws a square on the grid below. Three of the vertices are marked.

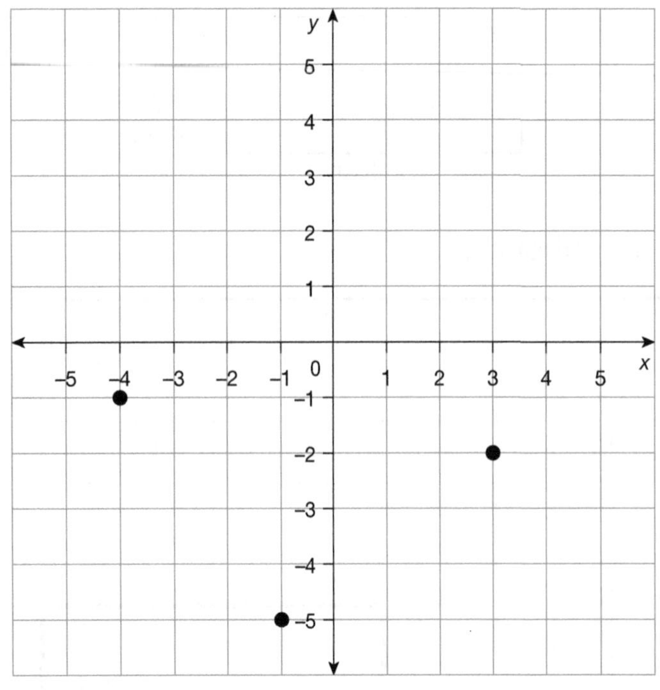

What are the coordinates of the missing vertex?

(,)

1 mark

9 In a sponsored swim, Connor managed 30 lengths. The total number of lengths covered by all swimmers was 45 times this distance.

What was the total number of lengths swum?

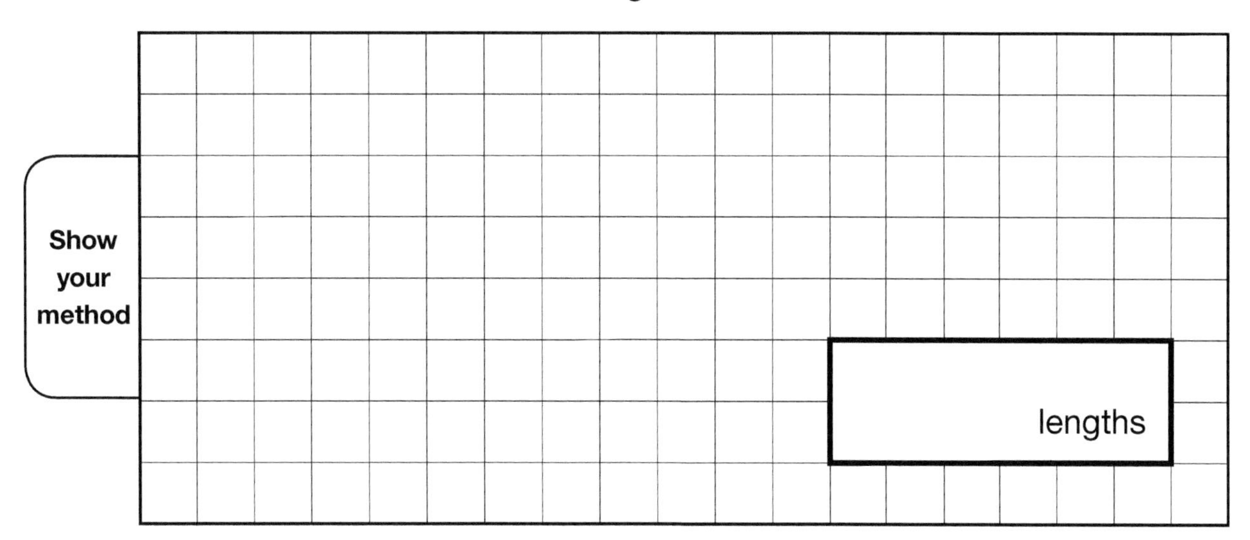

2 marks

Reasoning Test 6

1 A holiday on a cruise ship costs £3,999

Special offer
£1,100 off all holidays

How much is the cruise ship holiday with the special offer?

£ ______

1 mark

2 Felix is cycling a total of 368 laps of the school grounds for charity.

He has completed $\frac{1}{4}$ of the laps.

How many laps does he still have to complete?

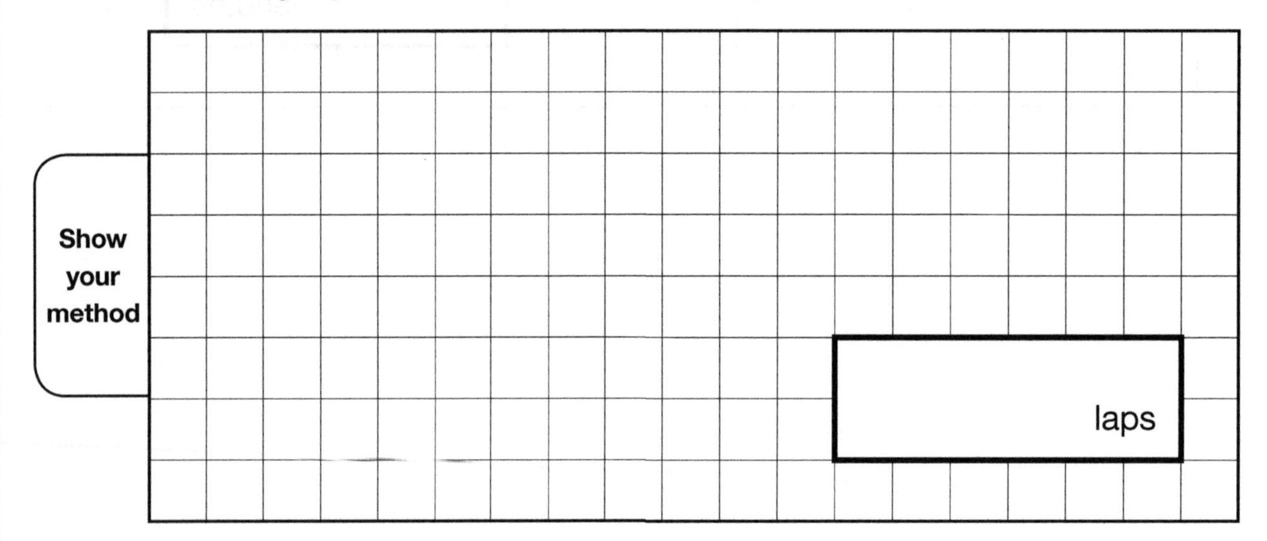

2 marks

3 Christy is making a box. Opposite faces of the box are the same colour.

Here is a net of her box. She has labelled the colours of three faces.

It needs one more green face and two red faces.

Write **red** and **green** on the correct empty faces on the net.

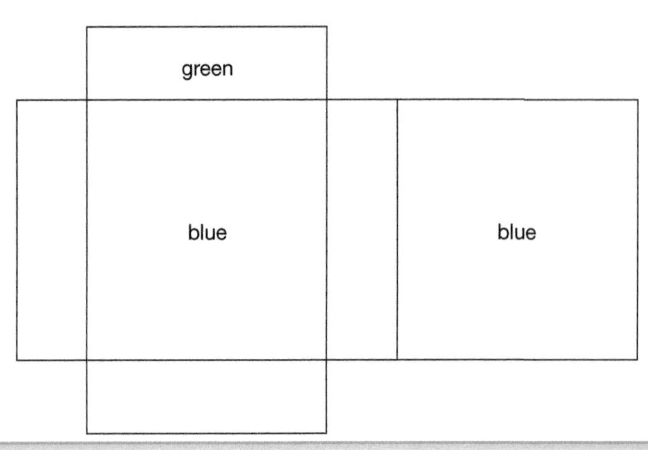

1 mark

4 The wheel of a car has a diameter of 72 cm

What is the radius of the car wheel?

cm

1 mark

5 27,450 = 366 × 75

Use this multiplication to complete the calculations below.

2,745 ÷ 366 = ☐

366 × 7.5 = ☐

366 × 750 = ☐

2 marks

6 Ava spends 6 hours at dance school each Saturday.

This is 25% of her total day.

On Sunday, she rests and sleeps for 18 hours.

Ava spends ☐ % of Sunday resting or sleeping.

1 mark

7 Daisy buys three packets of pencils.

Each packet costs exactly the same amount.

She pays with a £10 note.

Her change is £4.24

How much does each packet of pencils cost?

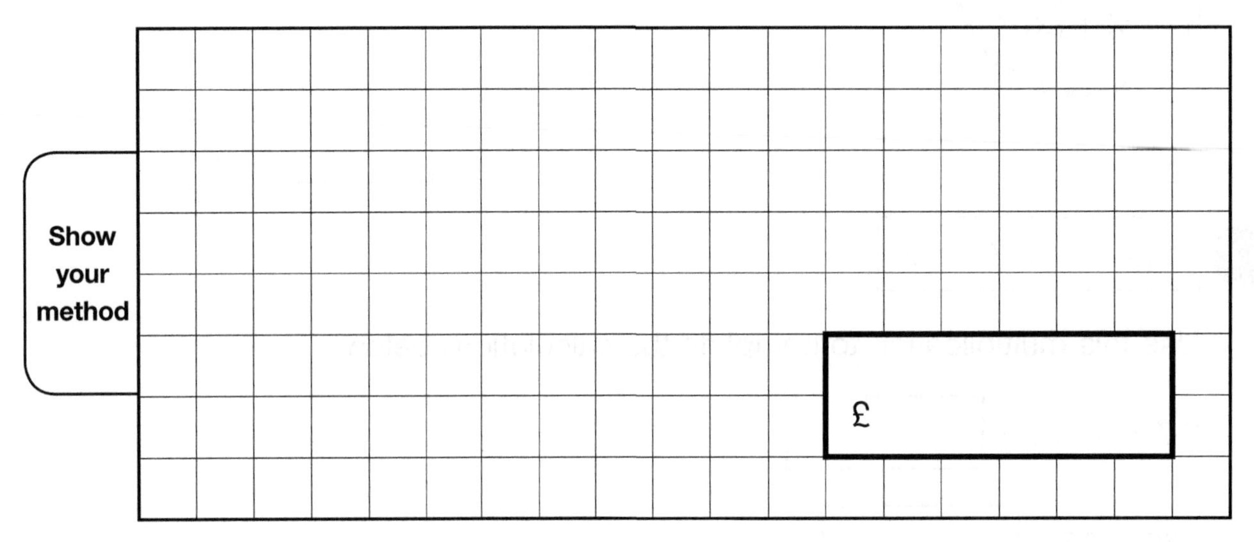

2 marks

8 Fakir bought four books.

Three of the books cost £6 each.

The other book cost £12.

What was the mean cost of the books?

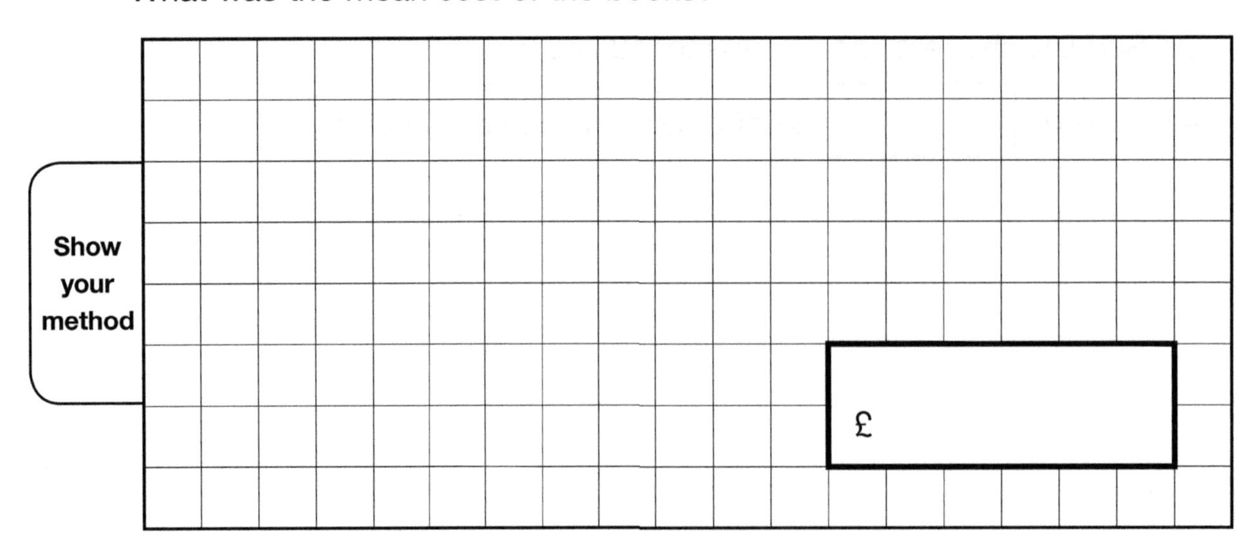

2 marks

Total marks .... /12

10 min

Reasoning Test 7

1 Kiki and Sam go on a trek with the Scouts.

Between them they have 2.7 litres of water.

Each time they stop for a rest, they drink 150 millilitres of water each.

How many stops do they make to drink until all the water is drunk?

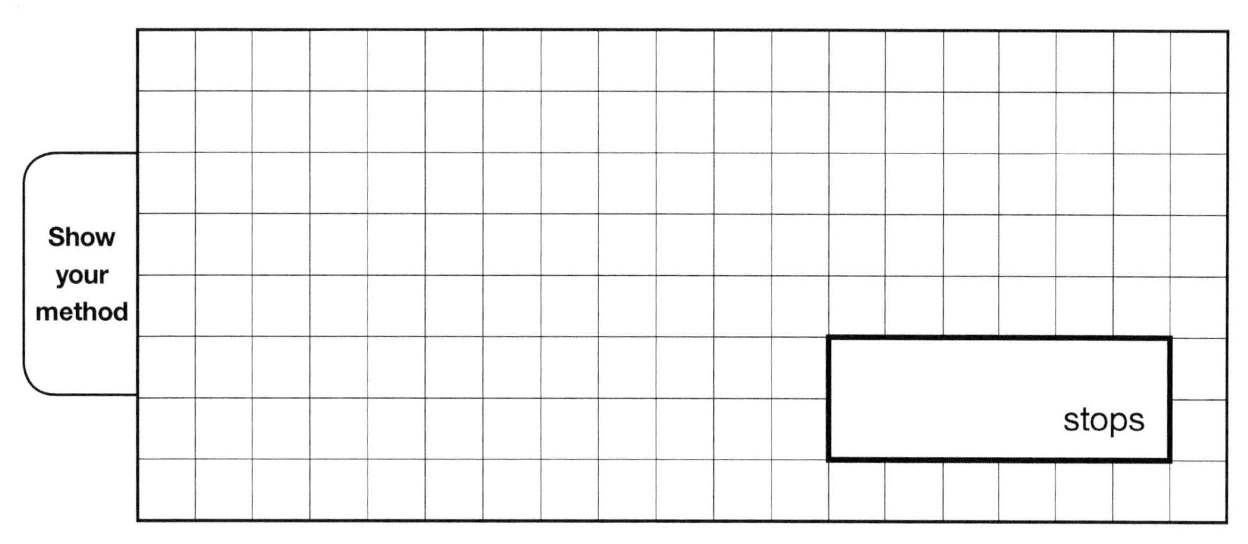

2 marks

2 Complete this multiplication grid with the correct numbers.

×	8	☐
☐	72	63
6	☐	42

1 mark

3 Chloe and Seamus share a pizza.

Chloe has 0.45 of the pizza. Seamus has $\frac{2}{5}$ of the pizza.

Explain who has the most.

1 mark

4 Emma's shop sells clothes, shoes and cosmetics.

Clothes are $\frac{2}{5}$ of the total sales.

Cosmetics are $\frac{1}{3}$ of the total sales.

The remaining sales are shoes.

What fraction of the total sales are shoes?

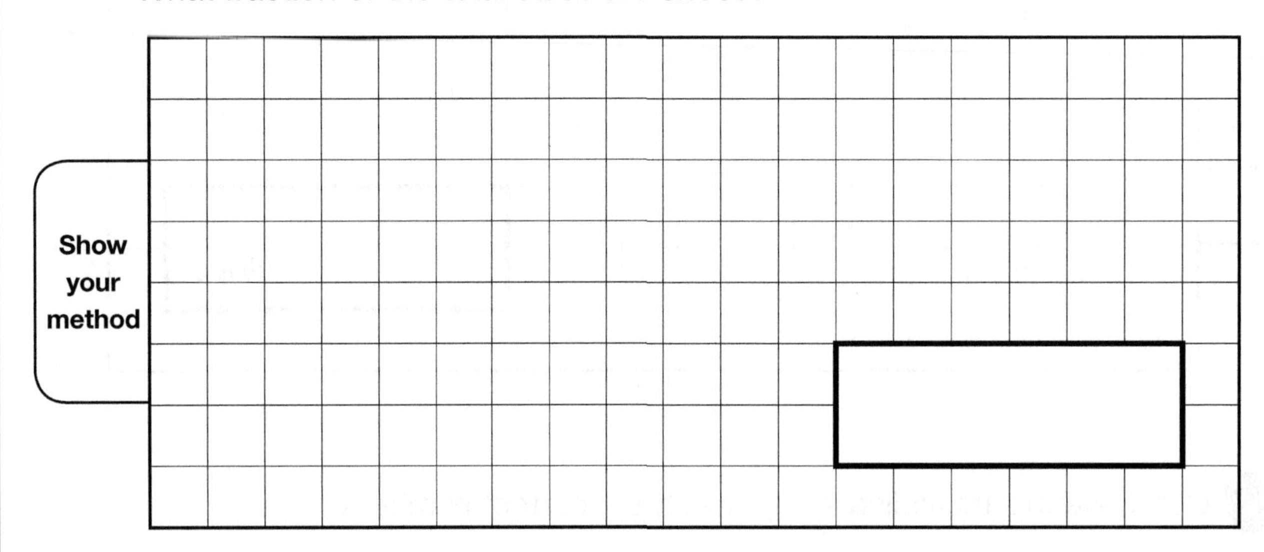

2 marks

5 A painting in a sale measures 35 cm in length by 20 cm in width.

Another painting is 5 cm shorter and 4 cm wider.

What is the difference in area of the two paintings?

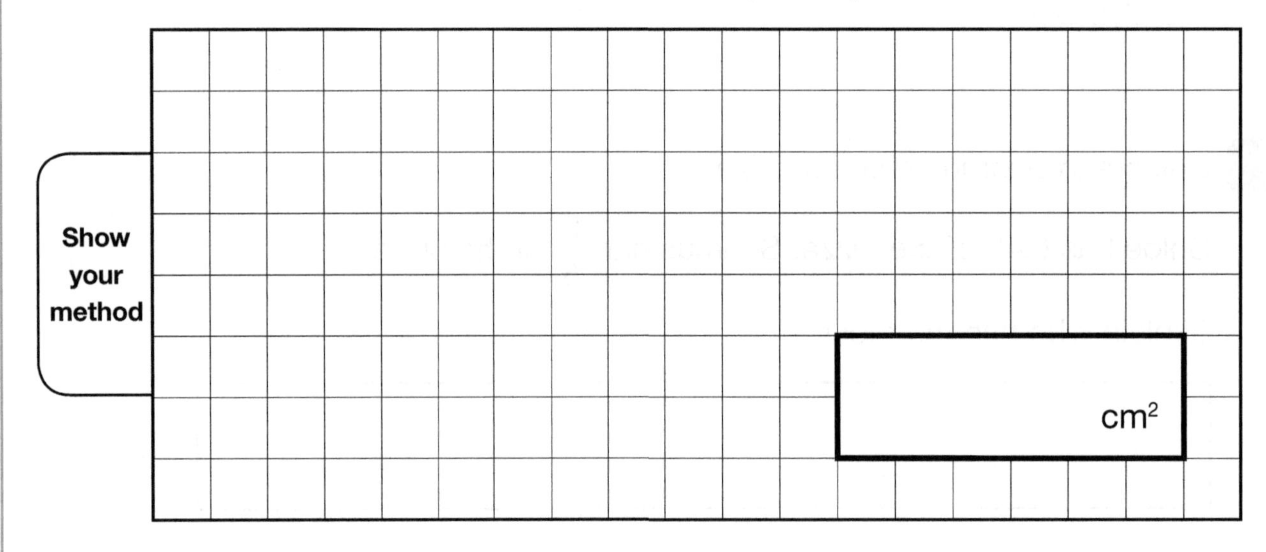

3 marks

6 Amir is estimating the answer to this calculation.

$4\frac{7}{8} + 2\frac{1}{6} - 3.9$

Tick the calculation that is the best estimate.

Tick **one**.

4 + 2 − 3 ☐

5 + 3 − 3 ☐

5 + 2 − 4 ☐

4 + 2 − 4 ☐

1 mark

7 Each box of chocolates has 2 layers.

There are 17 chocolates on each layer.

How many chocolates are there in 35 boxes?

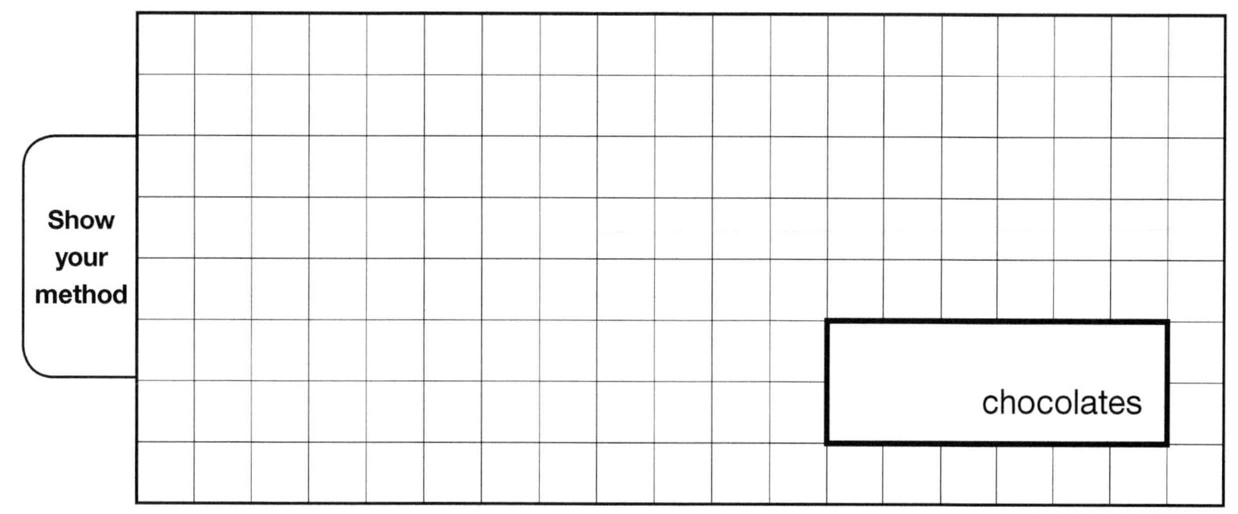

2 marks

8 Tick the shape which has the most acute angles.

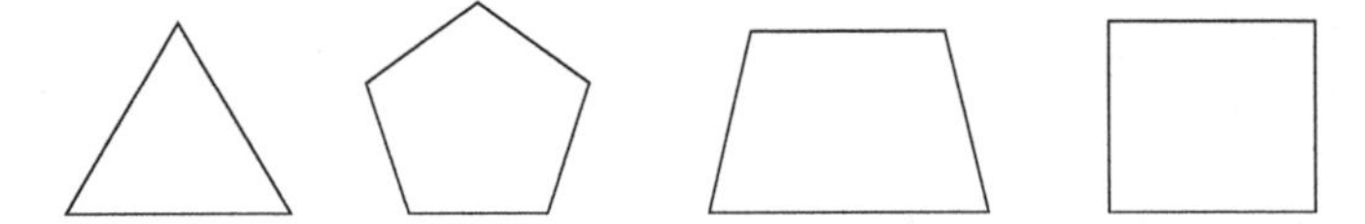

1 mark

9 The table shows the total weight of fruit thrown away by a supermarket over 5 days.

Day	Waste (g)
1	12,175
2	9,070
3	10,180
4	11,565
5	10,000

Saskia says,

Over 10 kg of fruit is thrown away every single day.

Explain whether or not she is correct.

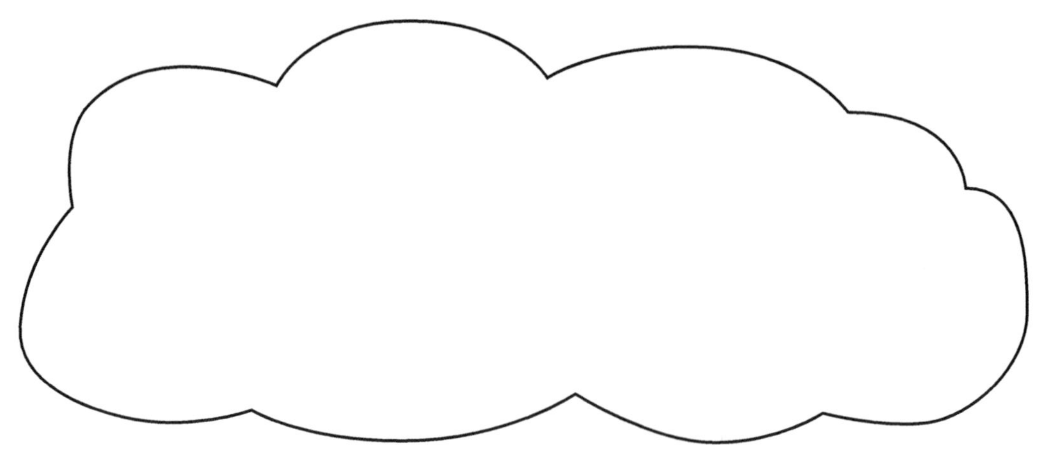

1 mark

Total marks .... /14

1 Each day in June, Molly runs either 3, 4 or 5 kilometres.
In the first 15 days of June she runs a total of 60 kilometres.

What is the greatest total distance Molly can run in the whole of June?

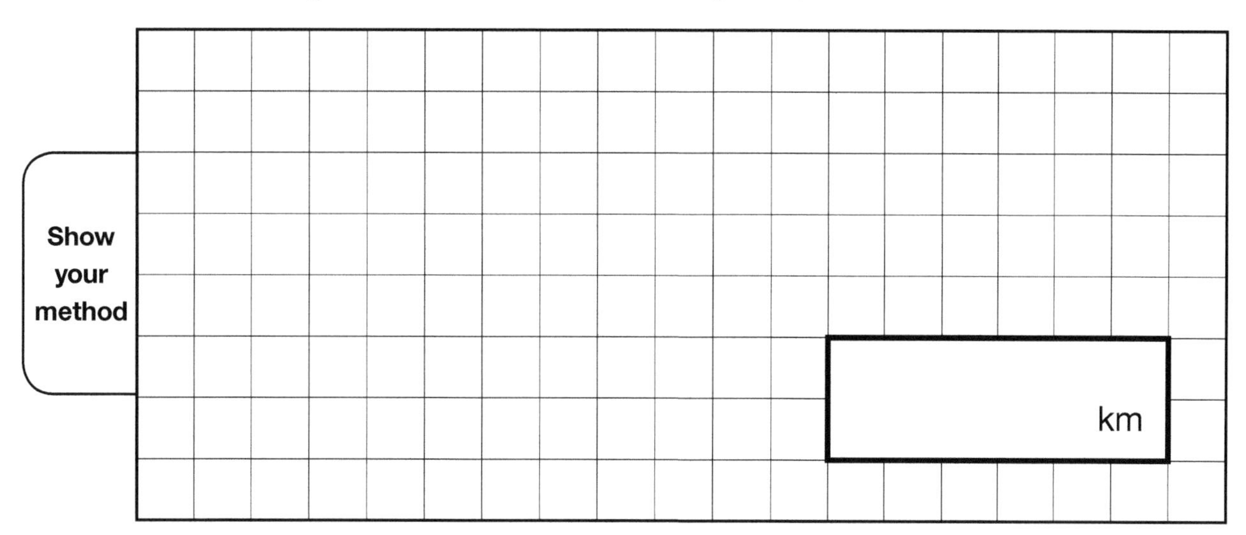

2 marks

2 A square number and a prime number have a difference of 6

The square number is less than 100

The prime number is between 10 and 20

What is the square number and the prime number?

☐ – ☐ = 6

square number – **prime number**

1 mark

3 Circle the greatest number below.

3.75 $\frac{12}{4}$ $3\frac{1}{2}$ $\frac{18}{5}$

1 mark

4 Write the missing digits to make this subtraction correct.

	☐	6	☐	7
–	2	7	8	☐
	1	8	5	5

2 marks

5 On a plan of a school, 1 cm represents 2.5 metres.

The perimeter of the playground is 65 metres.

How many centimetres is this on the plan of the school?

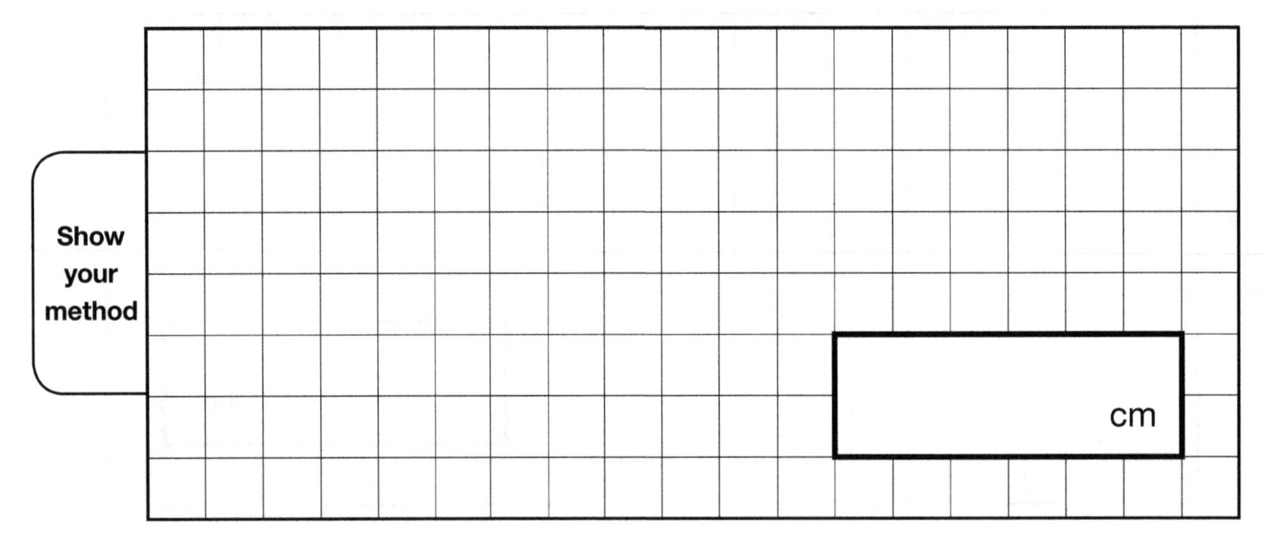

2 marks

6 James measures the radius of the roundabout at the park.

It is 1.2 metres. He says,

Explain whether he is correct.

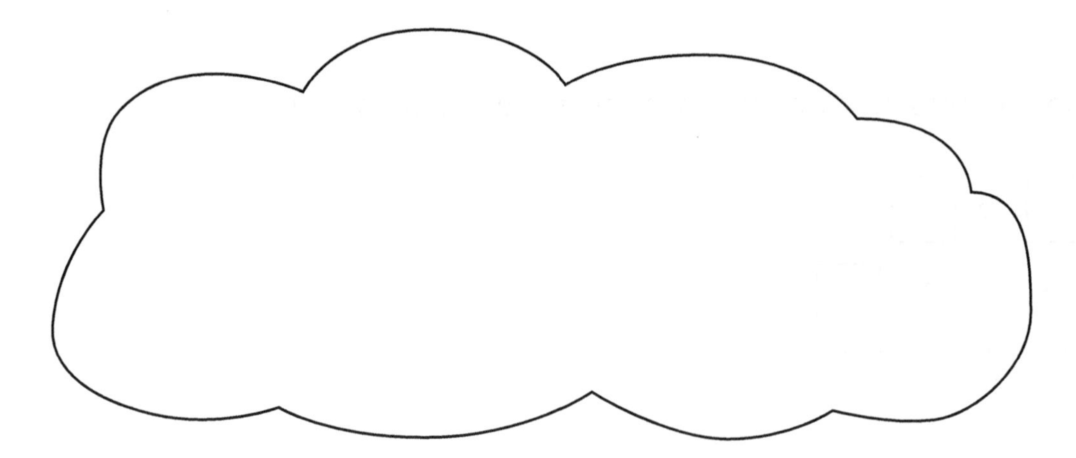

1 mark

7 How Many days are there in March, April and May altogether?

[ ] days

1 mark

8 Gaby is training for a triathlon.

Here is her training timetable for school days.

Time	Type of training				
6 – 7.30	Swimming	Running	Swimming	Running	Swimming
4.30 – 5.30	Running	Cycling	Running	Cycling	Running

What is her total number of hours of running?

[ ] hours

1 mark

9 Evie draws a quadrilateral. One of the angles is 110°.

She says,

My quadrilateral is a rectangle

Explain why she is not correct.

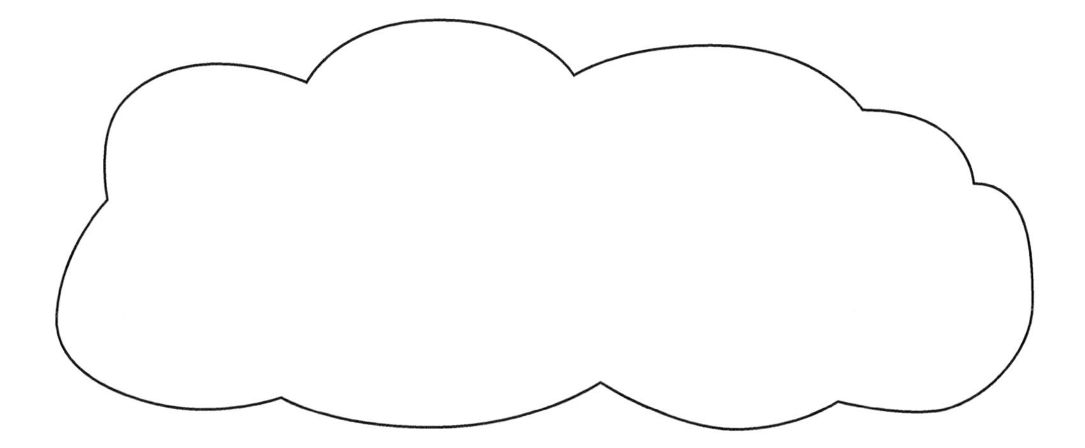

1 mark

Read the text below before answering the questions.

Adeena's Fire

As the clouds spread across the sky, Adeena's heart quickened. Her stomach churned as she wondered where the others had got to. It was becoming dark and a storm was approaching. Maybe they were on their way but could not see their small campsite in the failing light. Anxiously, she waited, but it was no use just sitting there. She knew she had to do something.

Adeena had an idea. If she could light the campfire, the glow would act like a beacon. It would also give her warmth. For the first time she noticed how cold it was getting. She hoped the others had been more successful in their search for food and had found more than her own meagre effort of a small bag of berries and an insignificant handful of seeds.

It was not easy lighting the fire but eventually flames rose from the pit. The heat and the extra light were comforting but there was still no sign of anyone approaching. Cracking twigs and rustling leaves sometimes gave Adeena hope but she quickly realised that these sounds were caused by the fire and small creatures. Any larger animals would hopefully be kept away by the flames.

By now she could no longer see the distant mountains, only the dark shapes of the nearby hills. The first drops of rain started to fall. Attempting to make the fire brighter, Adeena almost put it out with too many sticks. She began to sob: she was no longer just worried, she was also getting scared.

1 Look at the first paragraph.

What does *failing light* mean?

....

1 mark

2 Look at the second paragraph, beginning: *Adeena had an idea.*

What idea did Adeena have?

Tick **one**.

to look for the others ☐

to shelter from the storm ☐

to light the campfire ☐

to eat the berries ☐

1 mark

3 Look at the second paragraph, beginning: *Adeena had an idea.*

Find and **copy two** words or phrases which suggest that Adeena had not been very successful searching for food.

1) ....

1 mark

2) ....

1 mark

4 Look at the fourth paragraph, beginning: *By now she could no longer see...*

Why did Adeena start to sob?

Tick **one**.

She was hungry. ☐

She was scared. ☐

She was cold. ☐

It was raining. ☐

1 mark

5 Give **two** words or phrases that show that Adeena was successful in her attempt to light the fire.

1) ....

2) ....

1 mark

6 The text tells us that the fire helped keep Adeena warm and gave her light.

What are the other benefits of the fire lit by Adeena?

Explain your answer with reference to the text.

....

....

....

....

3 marks

Total marks .... /9

Reading Test 2

Read the text below before answering the questions.

The R101 Disaster

In 1930, the world was shocked when the R101 airship crashed killing 48 people. Airships were a pleasurable way of crossing oceans and continents. Passengers would dine and sleep in luxury as they cruised gently through the sky.

The R101 was huge and expensive. It had been built at Cardington in England. At over 200 metres long, it was a spectacular sight as it floated above the ground. It was built to compete with the Graf Zeppelin airship, which had already flown around the world, and the rival R100 which had flown across the Atlantic Ocean to Canada.

The airship was filled with hydrogen gas. The gas was stored in very large bags inside a steel frame. This was then covered with fabric. Hydrogen was perfect for lifting and keeping airships in the air, but it is also highly flammable and must be kept away from flames and heat. Safety would always be a concern.

On 4 October 1930, despite not being fully tested, it was decided that the R101 would fly to India. This would prove her capabilities to the world. Early in her journey she passed over London and then headed towards France. The weather conditions were far from ideal but it was felt that the R101 would cope with the heavy rain and strong winds. Unfortunately, near to the French town of Beauvais, disaster struck.

The R101 went into a steep dive. Although she hit the ground quite gently, some of the gas bags had been damaged and moments later caught fire. In no time at all the whole airship was alight. Of the 56 passengers, only eight managed to jump clear but two of those died from their injuries.

Special services were held to remember the dead. Memorials stand in the cemetery at Cardington and in Beauvais near the crash site. The Government decided to end the British airship building industry.

1 Look at the third paragraph, beginning: *The airship was filled with hydrogen gas.*

Which word is used to show that hydrogen gas can catch fire?

Tick **one**.

lifting ☐

gas ☐

flammable ☐

fabric ☐

1 mark

2 What phrase describes the weather conditions on 4 October 1930?

....

1 mark

3 What were the names of the R101's main rivals?

....

1 mark

4 Why do you think the Government decided to end the British airship building industry?

Explain your answer with reference to the text.

....

....

....

....

3 marks

5 *...cruised gently through the sky.*

What does this phrase suggest about travelling on an airship?

.... 1 mark

6 **Find** and **copy two** words from the first paragraph which suggest that travelling by airships was very comfortable.

1) .... 1 mark

2) .... 1 mark

Total marks .... /9

Reading Test 3

Read the text below before answering the questions.

Spotlight on the Stars

This week's star in the spotlight: **Zaney Z**

In the spotlight this week is Zaney Z, the instantly recognisable lead singer of mega group Zaney and the Zeds. Read on to find out about the real Zaney.

Favourite...

Clothes: Anything colourful and baggy. I like loose clothing because it's easier to dance in on stage. It also helps me keep cool. With all the movement and the spotlights, it gets very hot when we're performing.

Food: I love unhealthy food – pizzas, burgers, chips, crisps – but I only have them occasionally. It's important for me to stay fit and healthy because we do lots of training for our dance routines. I love a fruit salad for breakfast.

Biggest influences

My dad was a singer and I always wanted to be like him. He and my mum supported me by taking me to singing contests and they both come to most of my concerts in England. My mum is also my fitness coach so she's hugely important for our shows.

My main musical influences are Little Mix – they have such energy in their live shows – and Freddie Mercury. His voice, presence and his connection with the audience are things I will always aspire to. I wish I'd had the chance to meet him.

Hates...

Smoking: I hate the smell of it and it's really bad for you. People shouldn't smoke. Stay healthy.

People who judge me because they don't like my clothes or my music. They don't know me.

Big stars, big money

Zaney and the Zeds formed in 2016 when Zaney Z decided to ask three friends to join him in *The Midlands Find-A-Popstar* contest. Their performance was an instant success with over 4 million YouTube views as it became a viral sensation on social media. The group quickly became the hottest property in music and, by the end of 2017, they were embarking on a 124-show world tour. Zaney Z is one of the most recognisable stars in the world and, along with his group, earned over £40 million in 2018. Even if they don't gain any new fans, it is expected that by 2025 they will be the richest artists ever.

1 What **two** reasons does Zaney give for liking baggy clothes?

1) .... 1 mark

2) .... 1 mark

2 What does the text suggest will happen to Zaney and the Zeds in the future?

Tick **one**

They will become famous. ☐

Zaney Z will form a new band. ☐

They will become even richer. ☐

They will go on a world tour. ☐

1 mark

3 **Find** and **copy** the word in the *'Big stars, big money'* section which shows that the group were starting a world tour in 2017.

.... 1 mark

4 In the section *'Biggest influences'*, it says that Zaney will *always aspire* to Freddie Mercury's ... *voice, presence and his connection with the audience.* Tick **one** option below which is closest to what Zaney means by the word *aspire*.

Tick **one**.

He wants to be as famous as Freddie Mercury. ☐

Just like Freddie Mercury, he enjoys performing. ☐

It's his ambition to be able to perform like Freddie Mercury. ☐

Freddie Mercury was good. ☐

1 mark

5 Using evidence from the text, explain how Zaney feels about being fit and healthy.

....

....

....

.... 3 marks

6 What **two** things make Zaney hot when he is performing?

1) ....

2) .... 1 mark

Total marks .... /9

Reading Test 4

Read the text below before answering the questions.

Out for a Run

It was getting tedious. Three different TV shows watched while Mum was cleaning the apartment. I also did some colouring and drew a beautiful rainbow and unicorn, followed by several other pictures. I love drawing but not that much.

It looked lovely outside. The sky was a brilliant blue with small white clouds that looked like candy floss. Bright sunlight lit up the table and carpet, and I longed to be out there.

When Mum had finished cleaning, the apartment smelt as fresh as a summer's day. Mum said she was going for a run. I wanted to go with her. She looked at me as if I was a bit crazy but after we'd discussed it for a while, she said yes.

Down in the lift. Out of the apartment block. Into the fresh air. Start moving. Across the road. Past the bakery. Into the park. Rows of sweet daffodils. Birds in the trees. Feeling the wind in my hair. Across the playground. Waved to my friend and she waved back. Around the duck pond.

"Again," I demanded as we completed the lap. This time we went in the opposite direction.

Around the duck pond again. Another wave to my friend and another wave back. I loved the feeling of the air rushing over my face, hands, arms, body and legs. The birds still sitting tweeting on their branches. Rows of sweet daffodils, still blowing in the wind. Out of the park entrance. Past the bakery, which now made me feel hungry. Across the road again. Back into the warmth. Up in the lift. Mum seemed out of breath but I was ok.

The lift doors opened and Mum pushed my wheelchair the last few steps into our lovely clean home. Both of us smiled and both of us knew that we'd be doing this again soon.

1 Look at the first paragraph, beginning: *It was getting tedious.*

Which word is closest in meaning to *tedious*?

Tick **one**.

hot ☐

interesting ☐

clean ☐

boring ☐

1 mark

2 What had Mum planned to do after cleaning the apartment?

....

1 mark

3 What was the child thinking while watching television and drawing?

Tick **one** thought.

I don't like watching television. ☐

I'm a bit bored of sitting around in here. ☐

My drawings are the best. ☐

I want to help with the housework. ☐

1 mark

4 Why do you think Mum looked at the child as if she were *a bit crazy*?

Use evidence from the text to justify your answer.

....

.... 2 marks

5 Draw lines to match each paragraph to its main idea.

One has been done for you.

Paragraph	Main idea
Paragraph beginning: *It was getting tedious.*	the child wanted to go with Mum
Paragraph beginning: *It looked lovely outside.*	the child was having a great time
Paragraph beginning: *When Mum had finished cleaning…*	the child was bored
Paragraph beginning: *Around the duck pond again.*	the child wanted to be outside

1 mark

6 Explain how the author builds the story to a surprising ending.

Use evidence from the text to support your answer.

....

....

....

.... 3 marks

Total marks .... /9

Read the text below before answering the questions.

The Rain

Calm, sticky, humid air.
Silence but for a distant car.
The highway stretching infinitely ahead.
Dry, scorching concrete beneath bare, cracked feet.

Like a slow line of ants.
Making their way agonisingly onward.
No talking, shuffling footsteps.
Eyes heavy, mouths parched.

The first drops unnoticed by most.
But did someone feel something?
A slow but sure increase of chatter.
As they become certain.

On the surface now.
One, five, thirty and soon thousands of spots.
Water falling from the sky.
The excitement rising through painful limbs.

And then pouring.
Noisily, violently splashing down, roaring from above.
Lifesaving puddles cooling and drenching the road.
Bodies dropping, giving thanks through thirsty gulps.

1 Which line from the poem tells us that the road was long?

Tick **one**.

No talking, shuffling footsteps. ☐

Dry, scorching concrete beneath bare, cracked feet. ☐

The highway stretching infinitely ahead. ☐

Making their way agonisingly onward. ☐

1 mark

2 **Find** and **copy two** words or phrases that suggest that it was hot.

1) .... 1 mark

2) .... 1 mark

3 '*...shuffling footsteps. Eyes heavy...*'

What do these words from verse 3 of the poem suggest that the people were feeling?

....

1 mark

4 Which word in the poem is closest in meaning to the word 'dry'?

Tick **one**.

cracked ☐

parched ☐

scorching ☐

thirsty ☐

1 mark

5 Using evidence from the text, explain how it is inferred that the rain is very welcome.

....

....

.... 3 marks

6 **Find** and **copy three** words which tell us that the rain was heavy.

1) ....

2) ....

3) .... 1 mark

Total marks .... /9

Read the text below before answering the questions.

The Secret

The room had always been a mystery. We were never allowed in but we sometimes managed to peep through a crack in the door. Most of the furniture was dark wood – the floor-to-ceiling shelves and Grandpa's huge desk. Very-important-looking books with brown leather binding and gold titles I couldn't read stood in perfect lines, filling almost every space. The only hints of any real colour were the dark green telephone on the desk, a blue pen which lay next to it and the crimson leather chair where Grandpa would sit all day long, and sometimes all night long too. He would speak into his telephone, making notes and sometimes taking a book down from the shelf before making another telephone call. From his expression, he often seemed angry when he was in there but he talked in tones so hushed that we could not hear his anger. If he turned around fully and caught us peeping in, trying to hear what he was saying, the anger disappeared from his face and he'd gently wave and then shoo us away.

It was a windy and bitterly cold winter's evening when he invited me in. I'd been playing in the hallway, quietly as instructed. I'd heard a loud sigh from Grandpa's study and moved closer to the door. He knew I was there.

"Come in my child," Grandpa said, making me jump slightly.

I walked nervously to the door, opening it wide enough to fit through, hesitating until he reassured me that it was fine to enter. I remember running across the wooden floor and leaping into Grandpa's open arms and onto his lap. He talked to me but I didn't really hear what he said because I'd already noticed the one and only point of brightness I'd ever seen in that room. A drawer of the desk was open. Inside was a small golden box. It was metal and I knew immediately it was real gold. The box was also open, and inside I could see a paper scroll with a silver ribbon.

Grandpa knew I was staring, daring not to ask but longing to touch what was clearly something incredibly special. He reached out and lifted the box, taking my hand and letting me feel the impossibly smooth beauty of the gold. Grandpa told me not to touch the scroll, not yet anyway. He closed the lid and then told me many wondrous tales and secrets about the box, the scroll and the words it contained. I promised not to read the scroll until I was an adult, and promised not to speak of it until I had grandchildren of my own to tell.

I think I fell asleep there on Grandpa's lap because the next day I woke in my bed. I immediately remembered everything but knew I would tell nothing. Not until the time was right. I was the same person but I was now very different too. I had the secret. And it was a powerful one.

1 Which **two** statements about the story are true?

Tick **two**.

Grandpa had a green telephone.	☐
Grandpa was always angry.	☐
There was a golden box on the desk.	☐
It was winter.	☐

1 mark

2 Read the sentence below. What do the underlined words mean?

From his expression, he often seemed angry when he was in there but he talked in tones so hushed that we could not hear his anger.

....

1 mark

3 Which two related objects attracted the child's attention once he was in the study?

1) ....

1 mark

2) ....

1 mark

4 Explain why you think Grandpa invited the child into the study.

....

....

....

3 marks

5 *He closed the lid and then told me many wondrous tales and secrets about the box, the scroll and the words it contained.*

What impression does this sentence give about the box and scroll?

....

.... 1 mark

6 What was the child told not to touch?

.... 1 mark

Total marks .... /9

Read the text below before answering the questions.

Plastic – the Persistent Pest

Plastic is used in many different ways and has helped to shape our modern world. It is convenient and cheap to use for everything from vehicle parts to packaging, and from toys to building materials. But plastic is now widely recognised as a huge problem for our planet.

Devastating the Environment

Two of the major concerns are the amount of plastic we throw away, and the way it persists in the environment because it does not break down. Much of the plastic we throw away now will still be here in 1,000 years.

These concerns lead to further issues. Plastic is destroying the habitats of thousands of species of animals. Creatures are dying because they are swallowing, or getting caught in, plastic waste. It is having a devastating effect on the environment.

Poisoning our Seas and Poisoning Ourselves

The oceans are facing a huge problem with plastic. Research has shown that plastic waste can be found at depths greater than 10 km so much of it is never seen. However, vast areas of the surface of the ocean, some as large as countries, are covered in floating plastic – not visible from land but having a massive impact on the ocean environment. There are known to be at least five of these areas in the world's oceans, where currents bring together waste from around the globe. These areas can contain more plastic than prey, resulting in sea creatures eating plastic. If that is not concerning enough, many fish and other sea creatures eaten by humans have been found to contain plastic. Not only is plastic slowly poisoning our seas, but it could also be slowly poisoning us.

What can you do?

Environmental groups are determined to reduce the amount of plastic waste. Every minute, the equivalent of one lorry full of plastic enters our oceans. Campaigners say that we should stop 'single-use' plastics – plastic items that are used just once and thrown away – and find alternatives. This can include wrapping food in foil (which is recyclable) rather than cling-film (which is not). We are also encouraged to use alternatives to plastic bags when shopping. Putting pressure on shops and producers to reduce the amount of plastic packaging they use could also help. Rowan Brown, a long-term anti-plastic campaigner, says that together we can make a difference. "One or two people will not change the world but there is strength in numbers. If we all make an effort, if we all do our bit, then we can make a big difference for our planet, our children and our grandchildren."

1 *...we can make a big difference for our planet, our children and our grandchildren*

This suggests that solving the problem of plastic waste is...

Tick **one**.

quick and easy. ☐

for others to deal with. ☐

caused by children. ☐

a goal to achieve over time. ☐

1 mark

2 Complete the table below with **one** piece of evidence from the text to support each statement.

	Evidence
Plastic is harmful to wildlife.	
Makes the reader feel that there are things they can do to help.	

2 marks

3 Using evidence from the text, explain why the subtitle *Poisoning our Seas and Poisoning Ourselves* is used.

....

....

....

3 marks

4 Underline the word in the following sentence which means that plastic remains in the environment.

Two of the major concerns are the amount of plastic we throw away, and the way it persists in the environment because it does not break down.

1 mark

5 Tick two words that are used in the article to refer to the whole Earth.

Tick **two**.

surface ☐

world ☐

environment ☐

planet ☐

1 mark

6 Why does the author use words such as *devastating* and *poisoning* when referring to plastic waste in this article?

....

1 mark

Total marks .... /9

Read the text below before answering the questions.

Think Greatness

It's funny how traffic stops when you're in a rush.
Or how your hair's a mess but you can't find a brush.
The rain seems to start when it's time to play.
And you'd been wishing for a dry summer day.

It's funny how there's no bread when you want toast.
Or when you're tired and the puppy wants to play most.
You know that the baby will cry through the night.
When in the morning you must be early and bright.

It's funny how it snows but you must go to school.
Or when you want a warm bath but the water is cool.
Mum may have promised a day at the zoo.
But is called into work with so much to do.

So avoid disappointment and think in reverse.
It helps to make sure that things can't get worse.
If you never think great things could occur.
You'll never care that they …

But wait a minute, we all need to think greatness.
We need ambition, or we'd all be quite lifeless.
There should be no such word as cannot.
It's funny how our thinking can change a lot.

So think and dream and let thoughts be your guide.
Strap in and smile and enjoy life's ride.
Focus hard on what you'd most like to do.
It's funny how we can make thoughts come true.

1 In the final verse of the poem, what is meant by 'life's ride'?

Tick **one**.

We should ride everywhere. ☐

Life is like a journey. ☐

Life is very quick. ☐

Life is like a dream. ☐

1 mark

2 What does the poem suggest could be a problem when you want a warm bath?

....

1 mark

3 Which pair of lines in each of the first three verses are directly related to each other?

Tick **one**.

Lines 1 and 3 ☐

Lines 2 and 3 ☐

Lines 3 and 4 ☐

Lines 1 and 4 ☐

1 mark

4 What is similar and what is different between the first three verses and the final two verses of the poem?

....

....

.... 2 marks

5 What does verse four of the poem suggest you could do to avoid disappointment?

.... 1 mark

6 What message is given by this poem? Explain your answer by referring to the text.

....

....

.... 3 marks

Total marks .... /9

1 Which sentence must **not** end with an **exclamation mark**?

Tick **one**.

James was excited ☐

How did the children know ☐

There was a loud booming sound ☐

Aleeza was terrified ☐

1 mark

2 Which option completes the sentence in the **past perfect**?

Lena realised she .... over 10 kilometres when the challenge was completed.

Tick **one**.

was running ☐

run ☐

had run ☐

has run ☐

1 mark

3 Tick a sentence that uses a **dash** correctly.

Tick **one**.

They enjoyed – the windy weather it helped keep them cool in the sun. ☐

They enjoyed the windy weather – it helped keep them cool in the sun. ☐

They enjoyed – the windy weather it helped keep them cool in the sun. ☐

They enjoyed the windy weather it helped keep them cool – in the sun. ☐

1 mark

4 What does the prefix mis- mean in the words misbehave, misunderstand and mistreat?

Tick **one**.

carefully ☐

wrongly ☐

completely ☐

usually ☐

1 mark

5 Replace the underlined word in each sentence with the correct **pronoun**.

Mr Jones thought the netball team played so well that

Mr Jones allowed them extra playtime.

☐

When the players had finished their game, the players

realised how much effort they had put in. ☐

1 mark

6 Which sentence is written in **Standard English**?

Tick **one**.

Rossi seen the car in the distance. ☐

I done my running with my mum. ☐

Olivia played her guitar for her brother. ☐

We was going to watch the television. ☐

1 mark

7 Which punctuation mark should be used in the place indicated by

7 Which punctuation mark should be used in the place indicated by the arrow?

I enjoyed the film we watched last night ↑ the main character was amazing.

Tick **one**.

full stop ☐

semi-colon ☐

comma ☐

hyphen ☐

1 mark

8 What is the grammatical term for the underlined words in the sentence below?

Maya had <u>a bright red racing bike with blue and black lettering</u>.

....

1 mark

9 Which sentence uses the underlined word as a **noun**?

Tick **one**.

The <u>green</u> leaves were beginning to turn brown. ☐

Where is the town centre on the <u>large</u> map? ☐

There are lots of <u>rooms</u> in the old house. ☐

It was not very pleasant <u>seeing</u> them so upset. ☐

1 mark

10 Use a **subordinating conjunction** to show that the children played on the swings and then played with their ball.

The children played on the swings .... playing

with their ball.

1 mark

11 Rewrite the underlined verbs in the **simple past** tense.

The ducks and geese are able to fly away to search

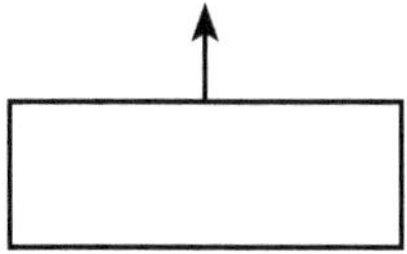

for food when winter comes to the pond.

1 mark

Total marks .... /11

10 min

Grammar and Punctuation Test 2

1 Read the sentence and underline the correct use of the word 'brothers' to show that more than one brother has a certificate.

I like to look at my **brother's/brothers'** dance certificates.

1 mark

2 Identify the sentence which **must** end with a **question mark**.

Tick **one**.

I will never know how they got there	☐
When we arrive, it will be dark	☐
Which direction should we travel	☐
She will find the way using her map	☐

1 mark

3 Which sentence shows that the class are most likely to go on a school trip?

Tick **one**.

The class might go on a trip.	☐
The class will go on a trip.	☐
The class may go on a trip.	☐
The class could go on a trip.	☐

1 mark

4 Underline the four **determiners** in the sentence below.

Each day an aeroplane brings a doctor to the island.

1 mark

5 Insert a **pair of commas** in the correct place in the sentence below.

Walking in the mountains even though they were several hours away was her favourite hobby.

1 mark

6 Insert an appropriate **subordinating conjunction** into the sentence below.

They carried plenty of water with them .... it was hot.

1 mark

7 Which verb form completes the sentence below?

After Alice .... into the water, she realised how cold it was.

Tick **one**.

had jumped ☐

is jumping ☐

has jumped ☐

was jumped ☐

1 mark

8 Underline the **main clause** in the sentence below.

Although it was dark, Jess was able to find her way through the forest.

1 mark

9 Which word is the **adverb** in the sentence below?

Tick **one**.

His fingers softly played each note as the stunned audience listened.

☐ softly ☐ played ☐ stunned ☐ listened

1 mark

10 Which sentence uses the **comma** correctly?

Tick **one**.

Silently, they watched the ships glide past the harbour wall.	☐
Silently they watched, the ships glide past the harbour wall.	☐
Silently they watched the ships, glide past the harbour wall.	☐
Silently they watched the ships glide past, the harbour wall.	☐

1 mark

11 Tick **one** box in each row to show whether the sentence is a **command**, a **question** or a **statement**.

Sentence	Command	Question	Statement
The water finds its way into streams and rivers.			
How long does it take the water to reach the sea?			
Do not waste water.			
Water is essential to life.			

1 mark

Total marks .... /11

Grammar and Punctuation Test 3

1 Which sentence uses the **colon** correctly?

Tick **one**.

They visited: many places the beach, the museum, the statue and the cinema. ☐

They visited many places: the beach, the museum, the statue and the cinema. ☐

They visited many places the: beach, the museum, the statue and the cinema. ☐

They visited many places the beach, the museum, the statue: and the cinema. ☐

1 mark

2 The prefix <u>dis-</u> can be added to the word <u>like</u> to make the word **dislike**.

Tick the meaning of the word **dislike**.

Tick **one**.

to like something even more ☐

to describe why you like something ☐

to not like something ☐

to like something a little ☐

1 mark

3 Use an appropriate **adverb** to complete the sentence.

The children ate their lunch ....

1 mark

4 Tick **one** box in each row to show whether the sentence is in the **past progressive** or the **present progressive** tense.

Sentence	Past progressive	Present progressive
Willow is playing her drums in assembly.		
Willow was playing her drums at the school concert.		
Willow is becoming a fantastic drummer.		

1 mark

5 Which sentence below uses the word clear as an **adjective**?

Tick **one**.

They managed to clear the mess. ☐

The children were in the clear. ☐

Above them was a clear sky. ☐

They were asked to stand clear. ☐

1 mark

6 Insert a **semi-colon** in the correct place in the sentence below.

There is no point shouting I will not change my mind.

1 mark

7 Insert a **comma** in the correct place in the sentence below.

Even when the snow became very deep outside the cottage was always warm.

1 mark

8 Tick **one** box in each row to show whether the **commas** are used correctly in the sentence.

Sentence	Commas used correctly	Commas used incorrectly
They ate bread and, jam sandwiches.		
Ishan can play the piano, guitar, flute and drums.		
Molly invited six friends, to her party.		
The church, with its large tower, was the tallest building in the village.		

1 mark

9 Which two sentences contain a **preposition**?

Tick **one**.

The car was on the motorway. ☐

Daisy was reading her book. ☐

We sailed past the island. ☐

James ate many sandwiches. ☐

1 mark

10 Rewrite the sentence below in the **active**.

The ball was hit by the tennis player.

....

....

1 mark

11 Which sentence is closest in meaning to the one below?

Ravi swims on at least five days each week.

Tick **one**.

Ravi likes swimming. ☐

Ravi wants to go swimming a lot. ☐

Ravi goes swimming more than four times per week. ☐

Ravi sometimes goes swimming. ☐

1 mark

Total marks .... /11

Grammar and Punctuation Test 4

1 Explain how the different **prefixes** change the meanings of the two sentences below.

The warning on the sign was unread.

This means that the warning on the sign ....

....

The warning on the sign was misread.

This means that the warning on the sign ....

....

1 mark

2 Circle the **conjunctions** in each sentence below.

Read the instructions before you make the model.

Be careful with the knife because it is sharp.

1 mark

3 Write the **simple past tense** of the underlined verbs in the boxes.

They were lucky they **catch** so many fish on their trip.

It was very hot as they **row** the boat and they

all **work** hard.

1 mark

4 Tick **two** boxes to show where the missing **inverted commas** should go.

☐ Most of the exhibits in the museum are from ☐ Egypt, ☐ said the museum curator. ☐

1 mark

5 Tick the option that correctly completes the sentence below.

.... had appeared in many dance shows.

Tick **one**.

During her childhood Mrs Smith, ☐

During, her childhood Mrs Smith ☐

During her childhood, Mrs Smith ☐

During her, childhood Mrs Smith ☐

1 mark

6 Which sentence uses the underlined word as a **noun**?

Tick **one**.

They are very <u>talented</u> children. ☐

Where is the <u>nearest</u> motorway? ☐

Every bike looked <u>expensive</u> and fast. ☐

The <u>wind</u> blew through their thin clothing. ☐

1 mark

7 Label each of the clauses in the sentence below as either **main (M)** or **subordinate (S)**.

As the swimmers entered the water, there was a huge splashing sound and the water became white with bubbles.

[ ] [ ] [ ]

1 mark

8 Circle the **relative pronoun** in the sentence below.

The long freight train, which stretched as far as the eye could see, carried food and timber.

1 mark

9 Draw a line to match each sentence to the correct **determiner**.

Use each determiner once.

Sentence	Determiner
There was .... icy mist over the lake.	the
In the tent was .... sleeping bag.	a
It was .... year he was born.	an

1 mark

10 What is the subject of the sentence below?

Next week, Abby wants to take her Gran to the theatre.

Tick **one**.

next week	☐
Abby	☐
Gran	☐
theatre	☐

1 mark

11 Add one **comma** to the sentence below to make it clear that Josh likes football and eating cakes.

At the weekend Josh enjoys playing football eating cakes

and seeing Grandma.

1 mark

Total marks .... /11

Grammar and Punctuation Test 5

10 min

1 Replace the underlined word in each sentence with the correct **pronoun**.

Petra was a very good singer and Petra could also play the piano.

Her piano had been given to her by her parents and the piano was very old.

1 mark

2 Complete the passage with **adjectives** derived from the nouns in brackets. The first one has been done for you.

It was very **dangerous** [danger] playing near the railway lines. The children had known this for a .... [length] time. They had watched a safety film starring a .... [fame] actor.

1 mark

3 Insert a **comma** in the correct place in the sentence below.

Stroking his beard the wizard came up with a cunning plan.

1 mark

4 Circle the **adverb** in the sentence below.

You must think fast if you want to win the quiz.

1 mark

5 Which verb completes the sentence below so that it uses the **subjunctive form**?

If I .... you, I'd try again.

Tick **one**.

was	☐
am	☐
are	☐
were	☐

1 mark

6 What is the name of the punctuation marks on either side of the words <u>who lived in Australia</u> in the sentence below?

Bella's uncle (who lived in Australia) sent her a toy snake for her birthday.

....

1 mark

7 Write a sentence using the word <u>sail</u> as a **verb**.

Punctuate your sentence correctly and do not change the verb.

....

1 mark

8 What kind of clause is underlined in the sentence below?

<u>Although they were already full,</u> they ordered a large dessert.

....

1 mark

9 Which sentence uses **capital letters** correctly?

Tick **one**.

They took a boat trip along the river nile in egypt. ☐

They took a Boat Trip along the river nile in Egypt. ☐

They took a boat trip along the river Nile in Egypt. ☐

They took a boat trip along the River Nile in Egypt. ☐

1 mark

10 Write a **noun phrase** containing at least **three** words to complete the sentence below.

.... was lighting up the night sky.

1 mark

11 Insert two **hyphens** in the correct places in the sentence below.

There were twenty six children in the class and they were all hard working and dedicated children.

1 mark

Total marks .... /11

Grammar and Punctuation Test 6

10 min

1 Circle the correct word in each box to complete the sentences in **Standard English**.

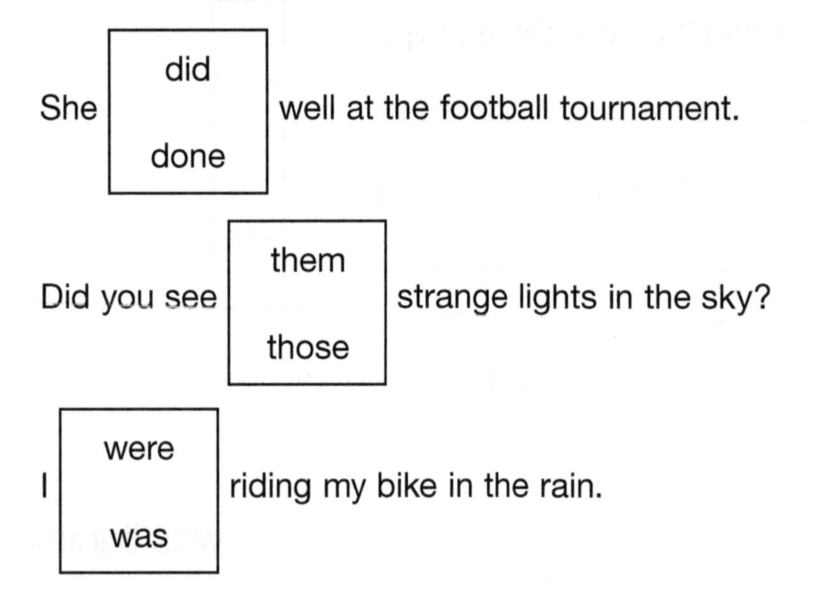

1 mark

2 Indicate the position of the missing **capital letters** in the sentence below.

In london, ava and rashid visited their friend jo and a museum.

1 mark

3 Draw a line to match each sentence to its correct **function**.
Use each function only once.

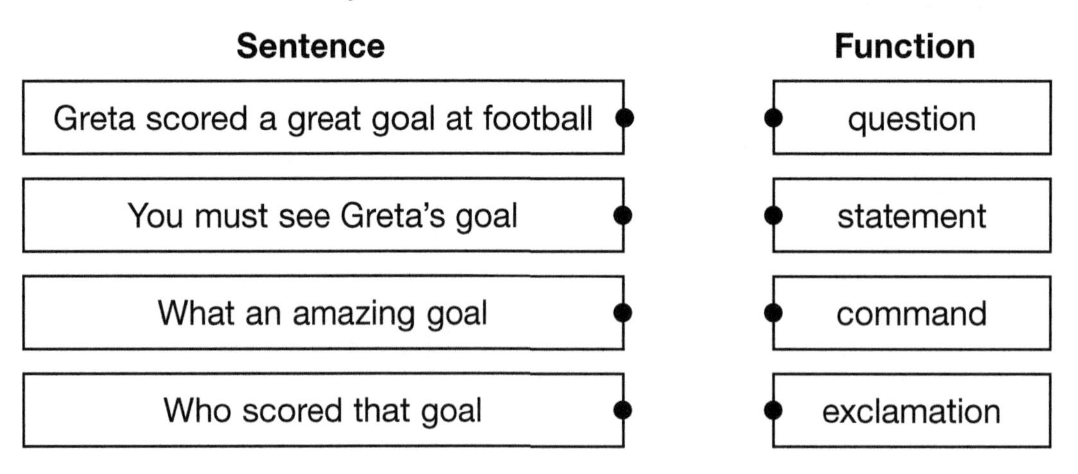

1 mark

4 Underline the **subordinate clause** in each sentence below.

The wind felt cold because they were dripping wet.

Although the storm was approaching, the fishing boats went out to sea.

1 mark

5 Draw a line to match each word to the correct **suffix** to make an **adjective**.

Word	Suffix
danger	able
like	ful
use	ous

1 mark

6 Which sentence shows that it is most likely to rain tomorrow?

Tick **one**.

It will rain tomorrow. ☐

It could rain tomorrow. ☐

It may rain tomorrow. ☐

It might rain tomorrow. ☐

1 mark

7 Circle the word in the sentence below that contains an **apostrophe** for **possession**.

If they'd only said they were coming, I'd have got the spare beds from Annie's shed.

1 mark

8 Which option correctly completes the sentence below?

The runner, ... won the race, was very fit.

Tick **one**.

whose	☐
which	☐
who	☐
whom	☐

1 mark

9 How are the underlined words used in the sentence below?

<u>Huge grey and black clouds</u> crept across the sky.

Tick **one**.

a fronted adverbial	☐
a relative clause	☐
a noun phrase	☐
a main clause	☐

1 mark

10 Underline the **relative clause** in the sentence below.

The lady who lives in the bungalow opposite was once a famous singer.

1 mark

11 Insert a pair of commas in the correct place in the sentence below.

Sara Jones who plays for United was voted the best footballer.

1 mark

Total marks .... /11

Grammar and Punctuation Test 7

10 min

1 What is the **word class** of the underlined word in the sentence below?

When they saw the suspect, the police <u>carefully</u> surrounded her.

....

1 mark

2 The prefix <u>re-</u> can be added to the root word <u>pay</u> to make the word **repay**.

Tick the meaning of the word **repay**.

Tick **one**.

to buy something ☐

to pay later ☐

to pay before ☐

to pay back ☐

1 mark

3 Which sentence is a **statement**?

Tick **one**.

Go there immediately ☐

What time do we leave ☐

It is a long way ☐

What a crazy journey ☐

1 mark

4 Underline the **object** in the sentence below.

The sea swept the whole family from the rocks.

1 mark

5 Circle the two **adverbs** in the sentence below.

They all watched the dancers silently but soon they were dancing with them.

1 mark

6 Which two pieces of advice will be useful to correct the punctuation in the sentence below?

We're home shouted Zak as they walked into the house.

	Tick **two**.
There should be a capital letter on 'shouted'.	☐
A comma is needed after 'home'.	☐
A question mark is needed after 'We're'.	☐
Inverted commas are needed around the spoken words, 'We're home'.	☐

1 mark

7 Complete the sentence below by writing the **conjunctions** from the box in the correct places.

Use each conjunction only once.

but	or	and

Go to the cake shop .... the bank, ...

don't forget to visit .... call Grandad.

1 mark

8 Which sentence has the most **formal** tone?

Tick **one**.

You can't play on that grass.	☐
That grass isn't for playing on.	☐
Playing on the grass is not allowed.	☐
You shouldn't play on the grass.	☐

1 mark

9 Insert two **commas** in the correct places in the sentence below.

Before they played netball Freddy Charlotte and Anika got changed.

1 mark

10 Underline the **relative clause** in the sentence below.

The cliffs which tower above the beach are very dangerous.

1 mark

11 Using each **prefix** from the box below only once, add one prefix to each word to make four different words.

re	im	in	mis

.... spell   .... correct

.... play   .... possible

1 mark

Grammar and Punctuation Test 8

1 Which sentence below is punctuated correctly?

Tick **one**.

How will we know whether it's the red, green or blue car. ☐

How will we know whether it's the red, green or blue car? ☐

How will we know whether its the red green or blue car? ☐

How will we know, whether it's the red green or blue car. ☐

1 mark

2 Which verb is a **synonym** of the verb <u>design</u>?

Tick **one**.

create ☐

build ☐

plan ☐

make ☐

1 mark

3 Which sentence uses the word <u>fire</u> as a **verb**?

Tick **one**.

They sat around the <u>fire</u> to keep warm. ☐

The <u>fire</u> raged in the forest. ☐

We had to <u>fire</u> the arrows at the target. ☐

Dad called the <u>fire</u> brigade for help. ☐

1 mark

4 Circle the **possessive pronoun** in the sentence below.

Raz said the ball was his but he could not remember who had given it to him.

1 mark

5 Which sentence is a **command**?

Tick **one**.

Eat everything on your plate ☐

Can you eat all of that ☐

Everything must be eaten tonight ☐

The plates must be cleared of all food ☐

1 mark

6 Circle the correct **verb form** in each underlined pair to complete the sentences below.

When we **was / were** on holiday, there **was / were** a huge swimming pool. The hotel workers **was / were** very helpful.

1 mark

7 Which sentence is punctuated correctly?

Tick **one**.

Jamal screamed stand back because, "I have no brakes!" ☐

Jamal screamed, "stand back because I have no brakes". ☐

Jamal screamed stand back because I have no brakes. ☐

Jamal screamed, "Stand back because I have no brakes!" ☐

1 mark

8 Complete the sentence below with a **noun** formed from the verb run.

At last the cross-country team had a fast ....

who would win races.

1 mark

9 Replace the underlined words in the sentences below with the correct **pronouns**.

Ella went to the theatre and Ella watched a great musical.

Ella's mum was with Ella.

1 mark

10 Replace the underlined words in the sentences below with their **contracted forms**.

We will see our friends and then they are going to the station.

I will not need to catch the train as there is a bus service.

1 mark

11 Explain how the **modal verb** changes the meaning of these two sentences.

If they win the game they become champions.

If they win the game they might become champions.

....

....

1 mark

Total marks .... /11

10 min

Spelling Test 1

1 They did not .... where they were going. 1 mark

2 The .... checked their car. 1 mark

3 When she closed her eyes, she got a strange

.... 1 mark

4 Jasmin was told to go .... to the school office. 1 mark

5 The oldest whale had the .... skin. 1 mark

6 It was .... to get colder as winter approached. 1 mark

7 The .... was useful to the police. 1 mark

8 They were the most .... shoes she could find. 1 mark

Total marks .... **/8**

10 min

Spelling Test 2

1 We had all .... the words to the song. 1 mark

2 They waved .... as the train left the platform. 1 mark

3 Jenny knew there was something .... about the old clock. 1 mark

4 A beautiful .... moon hung in the night sky. 1 mark

5 The kindness of others had made the day .... 1 mark

6 Wearing a hat was a .... decision. 1 mark

7 His .... kept him awake all night. 1 mark

8 The farmer had a huge .... of cattle. 1 mark

Total marks .... /8

Spelling Test 3

1 It was a very .... whale they spotted. 1 mark

2 There was a statue of a .... actress. 1 mark

3 They could find nothing to watch on .... 1 mark

4 Jack heard his voice .... around the cave. 1 mark

5 They were .... they would win the race. 1 mark

6 The car had always been very .... 1 mark

7 Everybody squeezed .... the gap in the fence. 1 mark

8 Nobody would .... her in this disguise. 1 mark

Total marks .... /8

10 min

Spelling Test 4

1 There were .... yellow lines on the road. 1 mark

2 He explored the ocean floor in a .... 1 mark

3 He painted a .... of the mountain. 1 mark

4 Each runner received a .... and certificate. 1 mark

5 Anything is .... with the right attitude. 1 mark

6 Cobwebs hung from the .... in the old ballroom. 1 mark

7 A special .... was needed to cross the river. 1 mark

8 She pulled a .... but still scored the goal. 1 mark

Total marks .... /8

10 min

Spelling Test 5

1. The whole family loved .... 1 mark

2. The pupils were asked to not .... 1 mark

3. The menu contained .... fish dishes. 1 mark

4. A ball was thrown .... in their direction. 1 mark

5. It was a tough .... to make. 1 mark

6. The .... needed much more practice. 1 mark

7. They all knew the .... so joined in. 1 mark

8. Sam had never seen such .... kittens. 1 mark

Total marks .... /8

10 min

Spelling Test 6

1 Charlie enjoyed reading the .... about the moor.

1 mark

2 Annie was a great violinist for a ....

1 mark

3 Long .... is often quite challenging.

1 mark

4 A .... incident was reported to the police.

1 mark

5 The school netball team won the ....

1 mark

6 The scientist had always been ....

1 mark

7 The creature made some .... rude noises.

1 mark

8 There was no .... that this was a great day.

1 mark

Total marks .... /8

10 min

Spelling Test 7

1 It was a fascinating .... to visit. ___ 1 mark

2 It was not windy .... to fly a kite. ___ 1 mark

3 They were promised great .... by the goblin. ___ 1 mark

4 They built a magnificent .... from junk. ___ 1 mark

5 Everyone was a little .... of his amazing voice. ___ 1 mark

6 An icy .... suspended itself over the lake. ___ 1 mark

7 Penguins are .... at swimming. ___ 1 mark

8 They were very .... in their research. ___ 1 mark

Total marks .... **/8**

Spelling Test 8

10 min

1 I .... it was raining outside. 1 mark

2 It was hard to .... how it used to look. 1 mark

3 There was a .... noise coming from the car. 1 mark

4 They were .... stuck until help arrived. 1 mark

5 A large .... was used to hold the rope in place. 1 mark

6 It was an .... to visit a new place. 1 mark

7 She hurt her .... when she fell off the bike. 1 mark

8 Yesterday we got a new ....。 1 mark

Total marks .... /8

Arithmetic			
Question	**Answer**	**Mark**	**Additional guidance**
Arithmetic Test 1			
1	200	1	
2	$\frac{7}{25}$	1	Accept $\frac{14}{50}$ as an equivalent fraction or the exact decimal equivalent 0.28
3	12	1	
4	840	1	Do not accept 840%
5	34	1	
6	770	1	
7	105,000	1	
8	Award **TWO** marks for the correct answer of 23 If the answer is incorrect, award **ONE** mark for a formal method of division with no more than ONE arithmetic error, e.g. 32⟌736 − 640 (32×20) 116 ← *error* − 96 (32×3) 20 32⟌736 − 650 (32×20) 86 ← *error*	Up to 2	Working must be carried through to reach a final answer for the award of **ONE** mark
9	$1\frac{7}{12}$	1	
10	74	1	
11	1,005	1	
12	$\frac{1}{20}$	1	Accept the exact decimal equivalent, i.e. $0.058\dot{3}$ (accept any clear indication of the recurring digits)
Arithmetic Test 2			
1	4,403	1	
2	$\frac{7}{12}$	1	
3	13.68	1	
4	$\frac{5}{6}$	1	Accept $\frac{15}{18}$ and other equivalent fractions or the exact decimal equivalent, i.e. $0.8\dot{3}$ (accept any clear indication of the recurring digits)
5	76	1	
6	$\frac{7}{20}$	1	Accept equivalent fractions or the exact decimal equivalent, i.e. 0.35
7	2,685	1	
8	105	1	

9	1.075	1	
10	Award **TWO** marks for the correct answer of 74,200 If the answer is incorrect, award **ONE** mark for a formal method of long multiplication with no more than ONE arithmetic error, e.g. 1325 **OR** 1325 × 56 × 56 7950 7940 *error* 66250 66250 63200 *error* 74190	Up to 2	Working must be carried through to reach a final answer for the award of **ONE** mark Do not award any marks if the error is in the place value, e.g. the omission of a zero when multiplying by tens, such as 1,325 × 50 = 6,625 (rather than 66,250)
11	Award **TWO** marks for the correct answer of 17 If the answer is incorrect, award **ONE** mark for a formal method of division with no more than ONE arithmetic error, e.g. 16r42 52 ⟌ 884 – 520 (52×10) 364 – 312 (52×6) 42 *error*	Up to 2	Working must be carried through to reach a final answer for the award of **ONE** mark
12	280	1	Do not accept 280%
Arithmetic Test 3			
1	72	1	
2	1,000	1	
3	1,841	1	
4	5.15	1	
5	60	1	
6	84	1	
7	1,324	1	
8	$\frac{3}{4}$	1	Accept equivalent fractions, e.g. $\frac{9}{12}$ or the exact decimal equivalent, i.e. 0.75
9	28.32	1	
10	$\frac{3}{10}$	1	Accept equivalent fractions, e.g. $\frac{6}{20}$ or the exact decimal equivalent, i.e. 0.3
11	132	1	Do not accept 132%
12	Award **TWO** marks for the correct answer of 86 If the answer is incorrect, award **ONE** mark for a formal method of division with no more than ONE arithmetic error, e.g. 86r2 42 ⟌ 3612 – 2100 (50×42) 1512	Up to 2	Working must be carried through to reach a final answer for the award of **ONE** mark

	– 1260 (30×42) 252 – 208 (5×42) *error* 44 – 42 2		
Arithmetic Test 4			
1	1,220	1	
2	$\frac{1}{2}$	1	Accept $\frac{4}{8}$ or other equivalent fractions, or the exact decimal equivalent, i.e. 0.5
3	3,937	1	
4	9	1	
5	52	1	
6	$\frac{1}{4}$	1	Accept equivalent fractions, e.g. $\frac{2}{8}$ or the exact decimal equivalent, i.e. 0.25
7	120	1	Do not accept 120%
8	61.12	1	
9	45	1	
10	424.2	1	
11	$4\frac{1}{12}$	1	Accept equivalent fractions, e.g. $\frac{49}{12}$ or the exact decimal equivalent, i.e. $4.08\dot{3}$ (accept any clear indication of the recurring digits)
12	Award **TWO** marks for the correct answer of 13 r 13 If the answer is incorrect, award **ONE** mark for a formal method of division with no more than ONE arithmetic error, e.g. 13r11 27 ⟌ 364 – 270 (10×27) 94 – 83 (3×27) *error* 11	Up to 2	Working must be carried through to reach a final answer for the award of **ONE** mark
Arithmetic Test 5			
1	271	1	
2	0	1	
3	12	1	
4	Award **TWO** marks for the correct answer of 7,638 If the answer is incorrect, award **ONE** mark for a formal method of long multiplication with no more than ONE arithmetic error, e.g. 402 × 19 3618 4020 7618 *error* **OR** 402 × 19 3608 *error* 4020 7628	Up to 2	Working must be carried through to reach a final answer for the award of **ONE** mark Do not award any marks if the error is in the place value, e.g. the omission of a zero when multiplying by tens, such as 402 × 10 = 402 (rather than 4,020)

5	220	1	
6	1	1	
7	35	1	
8	31	1	
9	0.602	1	
10	$\frac{1}{12}$	1	
11	2.75	1	
12	$\frac{11}{12}$	1	Accept equivalent fractions, e.g. $\frac{22}{24}$ or the exact decimal equivalent, i.e. $0.91\dot{6}$ (accept any clear indication of the recurring digits)
Arithmetic Test 6			
1	122	1	
2	7	1	
3	110	1	
4	$\frac{1}{2}$	1	Accept equivalent fractions, e.g. $\frac{9}{18}$ or the exact decimal equivalent, i.e. 0.5
5	$\frac{1}{3}$	1	Accept equivalent fractions, e.g. $\frac{5}{15}$ Accept the exact decimal equivalent, i.e. $0.\dot{3}$ (accept any clear indication of the recurring digits)
6	5.67	1	
7	30	1	
8	Award **TWO** marks for the correct answer of 60,320 If the answer is incorrect, award **ONE** mark for a formal method of long multiplication with no more than ONE arithmetic error, e.g. 928 × 65 4640 55680 60220 *error* **OR** 928 × 65 4540 *error* 55680 60220	Up to 2	Working must be carried through to reach a final answer for the award of **ONE** mark Do not award any marks if the error is in the place value, e.g. the omission of a zero when multiplying by tens, such as 928×60 = 5,568 (rather than 55,680)
9	100	1	
10	Award **TWO** marks for the correct answer of 24 If the answer is incorrect, award **ONE** mark for a formal method of division with no more than ONE arithmetic error, e.g. 23 37 ⟌ 888 − 740 (20×37) 148 − 148 (4×37) *error*	Up to 2	Working must be carried through to reach a final answer for the award of **ONE** mark

11	243	1	Do not accept 243%
12	$\frac{17}{24}$	1	Accept the exact decimal equivalent, i.e. $0.708\dot{3}$ (accept any clear indication of the recurring digits)
Arithmetic Test 7			
1	$\frac{8}{9}$	1	Accept equivalent fractions, e.g. $\frac{16}{18}$ or the exact decimal equivalent, i.e. $0.\dot{8}$ (accept any clear indication of the recurring digits)
2	322	1	
3	4,000	1	
4	8	1	
5	7,384	1	
6	3.641	1	
7	Award **TWO** marks for the correct answer of 85,504 If the answer is incorrect, award **ONE** mark for a formal method of long multiplication with no more than ONE arithmetic error, e.g. 2672 **OR** 2672 × 32 × 32 5344 5342 *error* 80160 80160 86504 *error* 85502	Up to 2	Working must be carried through to reach a final answer for the award of **ONE** mark Do not award any marks if the error is in the place value, e.g. the omission of a zero when multiplying by tens, such as 2,672 × 30 = 8,016 (rather than 80,160)
8	450	1	Do not accept 450%
9	$\frac{9}{10}$	1	Accept equivalent fractions, e.g. $\frac{18}{20}$ or the exact decimal equivalent, i.e. 0.9
10	$\frac{1}{25}$	1	Accept the exact decimal equivalent, i.e. 0.04
11	8,110	1	
12	1.548	1	
Arithmetic Test 8			
1	200	1	
2	70	1	
3	3.35	1	
4	9.632	1	
5	0	1	
6	5,600	1	
7	0.658	1	
8	567	1	
9	63	1	Do not accept 63%
10	$\frac{1}{32}$	1	Accept equivalent fractions, e.g. $\frac{2}{64}$ or the exact decimal equivalent, i.e. 0.03125
11	1,918	1	
12	141	1	

Reasoning

Question	Answer	Mark	Additional guidance
Reasoning Test 1			
1	Award **TWO** marks for: **Subtract 63 then subtract 13 ✓** **Subtract 6 then subtract 70 ✓** If the answer is incorrect, award **ONE** mark for: • only one box ticked correctly and no incorrect boxes ticked **OR** • two boxes ticked correctly and one incorrect box ticked	Up to 2	Accept correct answers clearly shown another way, e.g. circling, underlining
2	$\frac{75}{100}$ ✓ 0.75 ✓	1	Accept correct answers clearly shown another way, e.g. circling, underlining Both correct boxes must be ticked for the award of the mark. No additional boxes must be ticked
3	16 cm	1	
4	**a)** 150 **b)** 90	1 1	
5	720 degrees	1	
6	Award **TWO** marks for all three numbers correctly placed as shown: 81 **72** 63 54 **45** **36** Award **ONE** mark for two numbers correctly placed	Up to 2	
7	Award **ONE** mark for a point clearly indicated on the line within the range of 5.5 to 5.7 centimetres from the arrow	1	
8	**a)** £3.20 **b)** Award **TWO** marks for the correct answer of 6 toppings If the answer is incorrect, award **ONE** mark for the use of an appropriate method, e.g. • 200 – 30 – 30 – 30 – 30 – 30 – 30 **OR** • 30 × 6 **OR** • 30 × 10 = 300 – 30 – 30 – 30 – 30	1 Up to 2	Answer is not needed for the award of **ONE** mark
Reasoning Test 2			
1	0.4 0.423 0.43 1.004	1	All 4 numbers must be in the correct order for the award of **ONE** mark
2	75 – 32 = 43 **OR** 75 – 43 = 32	1	All 6 digit cards must be completed correctly for the award of **ONE** mark
3	Award **TWO** marks for 12 **AND** 13 **AND** 14 Award **ONE** mark for any two from 12, 13 and 14, and no more than one incorrect number	Up to 2	
4	Award **TWO** marks for the correct answer of 272 cm (or 2.72 m) If the answer is incorrect, award **ONE** mark for an appropriate method, e.g. • 90 cm – 56 cm = 34 cm, 34 cm × 8 =	Up to 2	Answer is not needed for the award of **ONE** mark

	OR • calculating the estimated length of each dinosaur from the two bones and then finding the difference		
5	27 cm^3	1	
6	Award **ONE** mark for the triangle completed as shown: (3, –3)	1	
7	Award **TWO** marks for all five factors: 1, 2, 4, 8 and 16 Award **ONE** mark for any three or four of the above, irrespective of any incorrect numbers	Up to 2	
8	Award **THREE** marks for the correct answer of 1.35 m **OR** 135 cm **OR** 1,350 mm If the answer is incorrect, award **TWO** marks for evidence of the correct multiplication (i.e. 350 mm × 29 = 10,150 mm **OR** 35 cm × 29 = 1,015 cm **OR** 0.35 m × 29 = 10.15 m) If the answer is incorrect, award **ONE** mark for showing that there needs to be multiplication by 29 (children) and subtraction from 11.5 metres	Up to 3	Answer is not needed for the award of **ONE** or **TWO** marks
9	3	1	
Reasoning Test 3			
1	207,040	1	
2	✓	1	Accept correct answer clearly shown another way, e.g. circling, underlining
3	Award **TWO** marks for all three correct as shown: 2 years = **24** months 56 days = **8** weeks 600 minutes = **10** hours Award **ONE** mark for two correct	Up to 2	
4	$\frac{19}{6}$ $\frac{18}{3}$ ($\frac{29}{3}$ circled) $\frac{27}{3}$	1	Accept correct answer clearly shown another way, e.g. ticking, underlining
5	2016	1	
6	**a)** 11°C **b)** –4°C	1 1	
7	Award **TWO** marks for both numbers correct as shown: $1\frac{1}{2}$ $1\frac{3}{4}$ **2** (boxed) $2\frac{1}{4}$ $\mathbf{2\frac{1}{2}}$ $2\frac{3}{4}$ Award **ONE** mark for one number correct	Up to 2	Accept decimal representation of $2\frac{1}{2}$, i.e. 2.5
8	Award **ONE** mark for the shape completed as shown: A (5, 5)	1	

9	Award **TWO** marks for the correct answer of £1.39 If the answer is incorrect, award **ONE** mark for evidence of an understanding that 82p should be multiplied by 9, and that £5.99 should be subtracted from this total	Up to 2	Answer is not needed for the award of **ONE** mark
Reasoning Test 4			
1	Award **TWO** marks for the correct answer of 180 If the answer is incorrect, award **ONE** mark for an appropriate method, e.g. • 36 + 36 + 36 + 18 + 18 + 18 + 18 **OR** • $(36 \times 3) + (18 \times 4)$ **OR** • 5×36 **OR** • 10×18	Up to 2	Answer is not needed for the award of **ONE** mark
2	Award **ONE** mark for the shape completed correctly as shown: mirror line	1	Accept slight inaccuracies in drawing Shape need not be shaded for the award of **ONE** mark
3	$\frac{6}{5}$ $\frac{5}{4}$ $\frac{4}{3}$	1	Accept the fraction joined to the correct box, rather than written in it
4	2 3 7 5	1	All digits must be in the correct order for the award of **ONE** mark
5	1,000	1	
6	$12 - a$	1	
7	Award **TWO** marks for: 7 children stayed in a hotel. ✓ Less then 50% of the children went camping. ✓ Award **ONE** mark for only one correct box ticked and no incorrect boxes ticked	Up to 2	No marks should be awarded if more than two boxes are ticked
8	Award **TWO** marks for the correct answer of 1,845 guests If the answer is incorrect, award **ONE** mark for an appropriate method which shows that 789 needs adding to the original total and 568 needs subtracting to find the new total (or that the difference between 789 and 568 needs adding to the original total)	Up to 2	Answer is not needed for the award of **ONE** mark
9	$x = 4$	1	
Reasoning Test 5			
1	✓ ✓	1	Both shapes must be identified for the award of **ONE** mark Accept correct answers clearly shown another way, e.g. circling, underlining
2	✓	1	Accept correct answer clearly shown another way, e.g. circling, underlining
3	20%	1	

4	Award **TWO** marks for the correct answer of 525 bottles If the answer is incorrect, award **ONE** mark for an appropriate method such as: • 3,200 – 750 – 1,400 and then dividing the answer (even if incorrect) by 2	Up to 2	Answer is not needed for the award of **ONE** mark
5	**a)** 19 degrees **b)** shed	1 1	
6	Award **TWO** marks for the correct answer of 4 cm If the answer is incorrect, award **ONE** mark for a clear understanding that the volume of a cuboid is found by multiplying the three dimensions, and that to find the missing dimension for cuboid, A, 15 (5×3) must be multiplied to make 60 cm^3 (the volume of cuboid B)	Up to 2	Answer is not needed for the award of **ONE** mark
7	Award **ONE** mark for an explanation that: • 0.6 is the same as $\frac{3}{5}$, which is smaller than $\frac{4}{5}$ **OR** • $\frac{4}{5}$ is the same as 0.8, which is bigger than 0.6	1	Accept similar reasoning using tenths, e.g. $0.6 = \frac{6}{10}$ and $\frac{4}{5} = \frac{8}{10}$ and then comparing
8	(0, 2)	1	Do not accept (2, 0)
9	Award **TWO** marks for the correct answer of 1,350 lengths If the answer is incorrect, award **ONE** mark for a method that shows that 30 lengths must be multiplied by 45	Up to 2	Answer is not needed for the award of **ONE** mark
Reasoning Test 6			
1	£2,899	1	
2	Award **TWO** marks for the correct answer of 276 laps If the answer is incorrect, award **ONE** mark for showing that a quarter of 368 needs to be found and subtracted from 368	Up to 2	Answer is not needed for the award of **ONE** mark
3	Award **ONE** mark for the three missing labels correctly placed as shown: green red blue red blue **green**	1	
4	36 cm	1	
5	Award **TWO** marks for all three correct answers as shown: $2,745 \div 366 =$ **7.5** $366 \times 7.5 =$ **2,745** $366 \times 750 =$ **274,500** Award **ONE** mark for two correct answers	Up to 2	
6	75%	1	
7	Award **TWO** marks for the correct answer of £1.92 If the answer is incorrect, award **ONE** mark for an attempt to subtract £4.24 from £10 to find the total amount spent (£5.76) and to divide this amount by 3 to find the cost per packet	Up to 2	Answer is not needed for the award of **ONE** mark
8	Award **TWO** marks for the correct answer of £7.50 If the answer is incorrect, award **ONE** mark for an attempt to find the total cost of the four books and to find the mean by dividing the total cost by 4	Up to 2	Answer is not needed for the award of **ONE** mark

<table>
<tr><th colspan="4">Reasoning Test 7</th></tr>
<tr><td>1</td><td>Award TWO marks for the correct answer of 9 stops

Award ONE mark for an incorrect answer with a method which demonstrates an understanding that the combined amount of water drunk at each stop is 300 ml, and that they need to find out how many times this goes into 2,700 ml (or 0.3 l into 2.7 l)</td><td>Up to 2</td><td>Answer is not needed for the award of ONE mark</td></tr>
<tr><td>2</td><td>Award ONE mark for all three numbers in the correct place as shown:
<table><tr><td>X</td><td>8</td><td>7</td></tr><tr><td>9</td><td>72</td><td>63</td></tr><tr><td>6</td><td>48</td><td>42</td></tr></table></td><td>1</td><td></td></tr>
<tr><td>3</td><td>Award ONE mark for an explanation that:
• Chloe has the most pizza because $\frac{2}{5}$ is the same as 0.4, which is less than 0.45</td><td>1</td><td></td></tr>
<tr><td>4</td><td>Award TWO marks for the correct answer of $\frac{4}{15}$

If the answer is incorrect, award ONE mark for showing evidence of finding a common denominator and converting $\frac{2}{5}$ and $\frac{1}{3}$ into $\frac{6}{15}$ and $\frac{5}{15}$</td><td>Up to 2</td><td>Answer is not needed for the award of ONE mark</td></tr>
<tr><td>5</td><td>Award THREE marks for the correct answer of 20 cm^2

If the answer is incorrect, award TWO marks for evidence of $(30 \times 24) - (35 \times 20)$ with no more than one error

If the answer is incorrect, award ONE mark for a clear understanding of the need to find the area of each painting and the difference</td><td>Up to 3</td><td>Answer is not needed for the award of ONE or TWO marks</td></tr>
<tr><td>6</td><td>5 + 2 − 4 ✓</td><td>1</td><td></td></tr>
<tr><td>7</td><td>Award TWO marks for the correct answer of 1,190 chocolates

If the answer is incorrect, award ONE mark for showing the need to find the number of chocolates in one box, i.e. 34 (17×2), and then multiply this by 35 (boxes)</td><td>Up to 2</td><td>Answer is not needed for the award of ONE mark</td></tr>
<tr><td>8</td><td>△ ✓</td><td>1</td><td>Accept correct answer clearly shown another way, e.g. circling, underlining</td></tr>
<tr><td>9</td><td>Award ONE mark for an explanation that:
• Saskia is incorrect because 9,070 g was thrown away on Day 2 and this is less than 10 kg (10,000 g)</td><td>1</td><td></td></tr>
<tr><th colspan="4">Reasoning Test 8</th></tr>
<tr><td>1</td><td>Award TWO marks for the correct answer of 135 km

If the answer is incorrect, award ONE mark for showing the need to multiply the remaining 15 days of the month by 5 km (the maximum daily distance) and add this to 60 km</td><td>Up to 2</td><td>Answer is not needed for the award of ONE mark</td></tr>
<tr><td>2</td><td>25 − 19 = 6</td><td>1</td><td></td></tr>
</table>

3	(3.75) $\frac{12}{4}$ $3\frac{1}{2}$ $\frac{18}{5}$	1	Accept correct answer clearly shown another way, e.g. ticking, underlining
4	Award **TWO** marks for all three numbers completed as shown: **4** 6 **3** 7 −2 7 8 **2** 1 8 5 5 Award **ONE** mark for any two numbers completed correctly	Up to 2	
5	Award **TWO** marks for the correct answer of 26 cm If the answer is incorrect, award **ONE** mark for showing the need to divide 65 by 2.5	Up to 2	Answer is not needed for the award of **ONE** mark
6	Award **ONE** mark for an explanation that: • James is incorrect because the diameter of a circle is double the size of the radius, and double 1.2 metres is 2.4 m, which is less than 3 metres	1	Do not accept an answer which does not show an understanding that the diameter is double the radius, and that double 1.2 m (or 2.4 m) is less than 3 m
7	92 days	1	
8	6 hours	1	
9	Award **ONE** mark for an explanation that: • a rectangle has four right angles (90°), meaning that a shape with a 110° angle cannot be a rectangle	1	Do not accept an answer which fails to acknowledge either that a rectangle has four 90° angles, or that it has four equal angles with a total of 360°

Reading

Question	Answer	Mark
Reading Test 1		
1	Award **ONE** mark for reference to any of the following: • it was getting dark(er) • the light was getting dim • it was not as bright as it had been • the clouds were making it darker. Do not accept 'it was night time'.	1
2	Award **ONE** mark for **to light the campfire** ✓	1
3	Award **TWO** marks for reference to two of the following: • meagre effort (of a small bag of berries) • insignificant (handful of seeds). • She hoped the others had been more successful. Award **ONE** mark for reference to one of the above.	Up to 2
4	Award **ONE** mark for **She was scared.** ✓	1

5	Award **ONE** mark for any **two** of the following: • flames rose (from the pit) • the heat and the extra light (were comforting) • sounds were caused by the fire • kept away by the flames • Attempting to make the fire brighter • Adeena almost put it out. Do not award the mark for just one example.	1
6	Award **THREE** marks for **two** acceptable points, at least one with evidence, e.g. • The fire would help the others find the campsite. (Evidence – it would 'act like a beacon') • The fire would protect Adeena/keep her safe. (Evidence – larger animals would be 'kept away by the flames'.) Award **TWO** marks for either **two** acceptable points, or **one** acceptable point with evidence. Award **ONE** mark for **one** acceptable point.	Up to 3
Reading Test 2		
1	Award **ONE** mark for **flammable** ✓	1
2	Award **ONE** mark for **far from ideal** Also accept **heavy rain and strong winds**	1
3	Award **ONE** mark for both **Graf Zeppelin** and **R100**	1
4	Award **THREE** marks for **two** acceptable points, at least one with evidence, e.g. • safety (evidence – 'Safety would always be a concern.', Hydrogen is 'highly flammable.') • cost of the R101 (evidence – 'The R101 was … expensive.') • to avoid further deaths/accidents (evidence – accept same evidence as for safety) • respect for those who died (no direct evidence in the text but could be inferred). Award **TWO** marks for either **two** acceptable points, or **one** acceptable point with evidence. Award **ONE** mark for **one** acceptable point.	Up to 3
5	Award **ONE** mark for any suggestion that: • it was smooth • it was comfortable • it was a pleasant way of flying Do not award a mark for 'gentle'.	1
6	Award **TWO** marks for reference to both of the following: • pleasurable • luxury Also accept **gently** Award **ONE** mark for reference to one of the above.	Up to 2
Reading Test 3		
1	Award **TWO** marks for reference to both of the following: • easier to dance in • helps him to keep cool Award **ONE** mark for reference to one of the above.	Up to 2
2	Award **ONE** mark for **They will become even richer.** ✓	1
3	Award **ONE** mark for **embarking**	1
4	Award **ONE** mark for **It's his ambition to be able to perform like Freddie Mercury**. ✓	1
5	Award **THREE** marks for an answer which suggests that because he is a performer who dances on stage he needs to stay fit and healthy, and includes at least three pieces of evidence from: • It is important to be fit and healthy when training for dance routines • He has a fitness coach • He says people shouldn't smoke • He only eats junk food occasionally.	Up to 3

	Award **TWO** marks for an answer that he thinks it is important to be fit and healthy, backed up by **two** pieces of evidence. Award **ONE** mark for an answer that he thinks it's important to be fit and healthy, backed up by **one** piece of evidence.	
6	Award **ONE** mark for reference to both of the following: • moving/movement (also accept 'dancing') • spotlights (also accept 'heat from spotlights').	1
Reading Test 4		
1	Award **ONE** mark for **boring** ✓	1
2	Award **ONE** mark for reference to Mum going for a run.	1
3	Award **ONE** mark for **I'm a bit bored of sitting around in here**. ✓	1
4	Award **TWO** marks for an answer which suggests Mum's surprise that the child wanted to go with her and the fact that the child was in a wheelchair. Award **ONE** mark for an answer which only acknowledges that the child was in a wheelchair.	Up to 2
5	Award **ONE** mark for matching all four correctly as shown: *It was getting tedious.* — the child was bored *It looked lovely outside.* — the child wanted to be outside *When Mum had finished cleaning.* — the child wanted to go with Mum *Around the duck pond again.* — the child was having a great time	1
6	Award **THREE** marks for reference to any three of the following, **TWO** marks for two and **ONE** mark for one: • The child wanting to go with Mum on her run, which makes the reader think the child was going to actually run with Mum. • The description of the run itself, which describes where they went and some of the feelings without any suggestion that the child wasn't running. • Reference to them doing the lap again. • Reference to Mum seeming out of breath, but the child being ok.	Up to 3
Reading Test 5		
1	Award **ONE** mark for **The highway stretching infinitely ahead.** ✓	1
2	Award **TWO** marks for reference to two of the following: • (Dry,) scorching (concrete) • (Calm, sticky,) humid (air) • (puddles) cooling (and drenching) Do not accept 'parched' or 'thirsty'. Award **ONE** mark for reference to one of the above.	Up to 2
3	Award **ONE** mark for reference to either of the following: • tired • sad	1
4	Award **ONE** mark for **parched** ✓	1
5	Award **THREE** marks for reference to any three of the following, **TWO** marks for two and **ONE** mark for one: • 'A slow but sure increase of chatter' which shows they were getting excited. • '(Water falling from the sky.) The excitement rising through painful limbs.' This shows they were excited that the rain was falling. • 'Life saving' shows that they needed it. • 'Bodies dropping, giving thanks through thirsty gulps.' This shows they were thankful that the rain had arrived/that they could now drink/that they could quench their parched mouths. Each answer must explain the words in the poem for the award of the marks.	Up to 3

6	Award **ONE** mark for any three from: • pouring • noisily (splashing) • violently (splashing) • roaring (from above) Do not accept 'drenching' as this refers to the puddles, not the rain itself.	1
Reading Test 6		
1	Award **ONE** mark for both: **Grandpa had a green telephone. ✓ It was winter. ✓**	1
2	Award **ONE** mark for an indication that he was talking very quietly/whispering. Do not accept 'they could not hear him' (which is already given).	1
3	Award **TWO** marks for reference to both of the following: • golden box • paper scroll Award **ONE** mark for reference to one of the above.	Up to 2
4	Award **THREE** marks for reference to all of the following, **TWO** marks for reference to three and **ONE** mark for reference to two: • to show him the box • to show him the scroll • to tell him about these items • to tell him that the items must remain secret (or so that he could pass the secret on/so that the child could become the keeper of the secret).	Up to 3
5	Award **ONE** mark for an answer which suggests that the contents of the box/scroll were very important and/or contained some special/magical words/powers.	1
6	Award **ONE** mark for **the scroll**	1
Reading Test 7		
1	Award **ONE** mark for **a goal to achieve over time.** ✓	1
2	Award **ONE** mark for any correct piece of evidence for each statement. Do not award more than one mark per statement. **Plastic is harmful to wildlife.** Evidence could include: Destroying habitats; Creatures are swallowing/getting caught in plastic; Plastic found in seas creatures. **Makes the reader feel that there are things they can do to help.** Evidence could include: Wrap food in foil; Use alternatives to plastic bags; Put pressure on shops and producers; Stop using single-use plastics.	Up to 2
3	Award **THREE** marks for an answer which refers to the seas being poisoned because there is so much plastic that it is getting eaten by sea creatures (reference can be made to 'more plastic than prey') and that plastic has been found in sea creatures eaten by humans, so it could be poisoning humans too. Award **TWO** marks for an answer which states that plastic is eaten by sea creatures and these could then be eaten by humans. Award **ONE** mark for an answer which refers to plastic being harmful to the oceans and humans if eaten.	Up to 3
4	Award **ONE** mark for underlining the correct word as shown: Two of the major concerns are the amount of plastic we throw away, and the way it <u>persists</u> in the environment because it does not break down.	1
5	Award **ONE** mark for both **world** ✓ and **planet** ✓	1
6	Award **ONE** mark for an answer which suggests that these words are used for impact, e.g. to get across how bad plastic waste is for the environment/Earth/oceans.	1
Reading Test 8		
1	Award **ONE** mark for **Life is like a journey.** ✓	1
2	Award **ONE** mark for **the water is cool/there is no hot water.**	1

3	Award **ONE** mark for **Lines 3 and 4** ✓	1
4	Award **TWO** marks for an answer which refers to any two of: • similarities in the use of the words 'It's funny how' • the same rhyming pattern. • the main difference is that the first three verses are about things not going right, but the last two are about being positive. Award **ONE** mark for one of the above.	Up to 2
5	Award **ONE** mark for reference to the suggestion that you think in reverse. Also accept 'think the opposite' or 'think things will go wrong'.	1
6	Award **THREE** marks for an answer which refers to: • the poem being about thinking positively even if things go wrong (and/or not accepting that things will always go wrong) • 'think greatness' (and/or 'we need ambition'; and/or 'there should be no such word as cannot'; and/or any other positive lines from the final two verses) • a comparison between the first three verses and the final two verses to evidence the positive message. Award **TWO** marks for an answer which refers to the poem being about thinking positively even if things go wrong, without any significant evidence from the text. Award **ONE** mark for an answer which only states that the message is about thinking positively.	Up to 3

Grammar and Punctuation

Question	Answer	Mark
Grammar and Punctuation Test 1		
1	Award **ONE** mark for **How did the children know** ✓	1
2	Award **ONE** mark for **had run** ✓	1
3	Award **ONE** mark for **They enjoyed the windy weather – it helped keep them cool in the sun.** ✓	1
4	Award **ONE** mark for **wrongly** ✓	1
5	Award **ONE** mark for using the correct pronouns as shown: Mr Jones thought the netball team played so well that **he** allowed them extra playtime. When the players had finished their game, **they** realised how much effort they had put in.	1
6	Award **ONE** mark for **Olivia played her guitar for her brother.** ✓	1
7	Award **ONE** mark for **semi-colon** ✓	1
8	Award **ONE** mark for **expanded noun phrase** Also accept **noun phrase**	1
9	Award **ONE** mark for **There are lots of <u>rooms</u> in the old house.** ✓	1
10	Award **ONE** mark for using the correct conjunction as shown: The children played on the swings **before** playing with their ball. The spelling of the word 'before' must be correct for the award of the mark.	1
11	Award **ONE** mark for using the two correct verbs as shown: The ducks and geese **were** able to fly away to search for food when winter **came** to the pond. The new verb form must be spelled correctly for the award of the mark.	1
Grammar and Punctuation Test 2		
1	Award **ONE** mark for underlining the correct option as shown: I like to look at my **brother's/<u>brothers'</u>** dance certificates.	1
2	Award **ONE** mark for **Which direction should we travel** ✓	1
3	Award **ONE** mark for **The class will go on a trip.** ✓	1
4	Award **ONE** mark for underlining all four determiners as shown: <u>Each</u> day <u>an</u> aeroplane brings <u>a</u> doctor to <u>the</u> island.	1

5	Award **ONE** mark for positioning both commas correctly as shown: Walking in the mountains**,** even though they were several hours away**,** was her favourite hobby.	1
6	Award **ONE** mark for using an appropriate subordinating conjunction, such as **since**, **in case, because, as**, e.g. • They carried plenty of water with them **because** it was hot.	1
7	Award **ONE** mark for **had jumped** ✓	1
8	Award **ONE** mark for underlining the main clause as shown: Although it was dark, Jess was able to find her way through the forest.	1
9	Award **ONE** mark for ticking the adverb as shown: His fingers softly played each note as the stunned audience listened. (✓ under softly)	1
10	Award **ONE** mark for **Silently, they watched the ships glide past the harbour wall.** ✓	1
11	Award **ONE** mark for all four ticks correctly placed as shown:	1

Sentence	Command	Question	Statement
The water finds its way into streams and rivers.			✓
How long does it take the water to reach the sea?		✓	
Do not waste water.	✓		
Water is essential to life.			✓

Grammar and Punctuation Test 3

1	Award **ONE** mark for **They visited many places: the beach, the museum, the statue and the cinema.** ✓	1
2	Award **ONE** mark for **to not like something** ✓	1
3	Award **ONE** mark for using an appropriate adverb, such as **quickly, slowly, silently, later, yesterday**, e.g. • The children ate their lunch **quickly**. The spelling of the adverb must be correct for the award of the mark.	1
4	Award **ONE** mark for all three ticks correctly placed as shown:	1

Sentence	Past	Present
Willow is playing her drums in assembly.		✓
Willow was playing her drums at the school concert.	✓	
Willow is becoming a fantastic drummer.		✓

5	Award **ONE** mark for **Above them was a clear sky.** ✓	1
6	Award **ONE** mark for positioning the semi-colon correctly as shown: There is no point shouting**;** I will not change my mind.	1
7	Award **ONE** mark for positioning the comma correctly as shown: Even when the snow became very deep outside**,** the cottage was always warm.	1
8	Award **ONE** mark for all four ticks placed correctly as shown:	1

Sentence	Used correctly	Used incorrectly
They ate bread and, jam sandwiches.		✓
Ishan can play the piano, guitar, flute and drums.	✓	
Molly invited six friends, to her party.		✓
The church, with its large tower, was the tallest building in the village.	✓	

9	Award **ONE** mark for **The car was on the motorway.** ✓ and **We sailed past the island.** ✓	1

10	Award **ONE** mark for writing the sentence in the active as shown: **The tennis player hit the ball.** Do not accept misspellings or incorrect punctuation.	1
11	Award **ONE** mark for **Ravi goes swimming more than four times per week.** ✓	1
Grammar and Punctuation Test 4		
1	Award **ONE** mark for a suitable explanation of both sentences, e.g. • unread = This means that the warning on the sign *had not been read.* • misread = This means that the warning on the sign *had been read incorrectly.*	1
2	Award **ONE** mark for circling both conjunctions as shown: Read the instructions (before) you make the model. Be careful with the knife (because) it is sharp.	1
3	Award **ONE** mark for using all three correct verbs as shown: They were lucky they **caught** so many fish on their trip. It was very hot as they **rowed** the boat and they all **worked** hard.	1
4	Award **ONE** mark for ticking both boxes correctly: ✓ ✓ Most of the exhibits in the museum are from Egypt, said the museum curator.	1
5	Award **ONE** mark for **During her childhood, Mrs Smith** ✓	1
6	Award **ONE** mark for **The wind blew through their thin clothing.** ✓	1
7	Award **ONE** mark for labelling all three clauses correctly as shown: As the swimmers entered the water, there was a huge splashing sound and the water became white with bubbles. M S M	1
8	Award **ONE** mark for circling the relative pronoun as shown: The long freight train, (which) stretched as far as the eye could see, carried food and timber.	1
9	Award **ONE** mark for matching all three as shown: There was ___ icy mist over the lake. — an In the tent was ___ sleeping bag. — a It was _____ year he was born. — the	1
10	Award **ONE** mark for **Abby** ✓	1
11	Award **ONE** mark for positioning the comma correctly as shown: At the weekend Josh enjoys playing football**,** eating cakes and seeing Grandma.	1
Grammar and Punctuation Test 5		
1	Award **ONE** mark for using the correct pronouns as shown: Petra was a very good singer and **she** could also play the piano. Her piano had been given to her by her parents and **it** was very old.	1
2	Award **ONE** mark for adding both adjectives correctly as shown: It was very dangerous playing near the railway lines. The children had known this for a **long** time. They had watched a safety film starring a **famous** actor.	1
3	Award **ONE** mark for positioning the comma correctly as shown: Stroking his beard**,** the wizard came up with a cunning plan.	1
4	Award **ONE** mark for circling the adverb correctly as shown: You must think (fast) if you want to win the quiz.	1
5	Award **ONE** mark for **were** ✓	1
6	Award **ONE** mark for **brackets** or **pair of brackets**	1

7	Award **ONE** mark for a grammatically correct sentence that uses 'sail' as a verb and that is correctly punctuated, e.g. • **We sail our boat each weekend.** • **The birds sail past on the wind.** Do not award a mark for incorrect punctuation or changes to the word sail.	1
8	Award **ONE** mark for **subordinate clause.**	1
9	Award **ONE** mark for **They took a boat trip along the River Nile in Egypt.** ✓	1
10	Award **ONE** mark for an appropriate noun phrase of three or more words, e.g. • **A spectacular moon** was lighting up the night sky. • **The bright moon** was lighting up the night sky. • **A beautiful firework display** was lighting up the night sky.	1
11	Award **ONE** mark for positioning the two hyphens correctly as shown: There were twenty-six children in the class and they were all hard-working and dedicated children.	1
Grammar and Punctuation Test 6		
1	Award **ONE** mark for circling the correct words: **did; those; was**	1
2	Award **ONE** mark for circling all four missing capital letters as shown: In (l)ondon, (a)va and (r)ashid visited their friend (j)o and a museum.	1
3	Award **ONE** mark for matching all four correctly as shown: Greta scored a great goal at football — question You must see Greta's goal — statement What an amazing goal — command Who scored that goal — exclamation	1
4	Award **ONE** mark for underlining both subordinate clauses correctly as shown: The wind felt cold because they were dripping wet. Although the storm was approaching, the fishing boats went out to sea.	1
5	Award **ONE** mark for matching all three correctly as shown: danger — able like — ful use — ous	1
6	Award **ONE** mark for **It will rain tomorrow**. ✓	1
7	Award **ONE** mark for circling the correct word as shown: If they'd only said they were coming, I'd have got the spare beds from (Annie's) shed.	1
8	Award **ONE** mark for **who** ✓	1
9	Award **ONE** mark for **a noun phrase** ✓	1
10	Award **ONE** mark for underlining the relative clause as shown: The lady who lives in the bungalow opposite was once a famous singer.	1
11	Award **ONE** mark for positioning the two commas correctly as shown: Sara Jones**,** who plays for United**,** was voted the best footballer.	1
Grammar and Punctuation Test 7		
1	Award **ONE** mark for **adverb**	1
2	Award **ONE** mark for **to pay back** ✓	1
3	Award **ONE** mark for **It is a long way** ✓	1
4	Award **ONE** mark for underlining the object correctly as shown: The sea swept the whole family from the rocks. Also accept 'The sea swept the whole family from the rocks.'	1
5	Award **ONE** mark for circling the two adverbs as shown: They all watched the dancers (silently) but (soon) they were dancing with them.	1

6	Award **ONE** mark for **A comma is needed after 'home'.** ✓ and **Inverted commas are needed around the spoken words, 'We're home'.** ✓	1
7	Award **ONE** mark for using all three conjunctions correctly as shown: Go to the cake shop **and** the bank, **but** don't forget to visit **or** call Grandad.	1
8	Award **ONE** mark for **Playing on the grass is not allowed.** ✓	1
9	Award **ONE** mark for positioning both commas correctly as shown: Before they played netball**,** Freddy**,** Charlotte and Anika got changed.	1
10	Award **ONE** mark for underlining the relative clause correctly as shown: The cliffs which tower above the beach are very dangerous.	1
11	Award **ONE** mark for using all four prefixes correctly as shown: **mis**spell, **in**correct, **re**play, **im**possible	1
Grammar and Punctuation Test 8		
1	Award **ONE** mark for **How will we know whether it's the red, green or blue car**? ✓	1
2	Award **ONE** mark for **plan** ✓	1
3	Award **ONE** mark for **We had to fire the arrows at the target.** ✓	1
4	Award **ONE** mark for circling the possessive pronoun as shown: Raz said the ball was (his) but he could not remember who had given it to him.	1
5	Award **ONE** mark for **Eat everything on your plate** ✓	1
6	Award **ONE** mark for circling the three correct verb forms as shown: When we **was/(were)** on holiday, there **(was)/were** a huge swimming pool. The hotel workers **was/(were)** very helpful.	1
7	Award **ONE** mark for **Jamal screamed, "Stand back because I have no brakes!"** ✓	1
8	Award **ONE** mark for using the correct noun form as shown: At last the cross-country team had a fast **runner** who would win races.	1
9	Award **ONE** mark for the correct pronouns: Ella went to the theatre and **she** watched a great musical. Ella's mum was with **her**.	1
10	Award **ONE** mark for the correct contracted forms: **We'll** see our friends and then **they're** going to the station. I **won't** need to catch the train as there is a bus service.	1
11	Award **ONE** mark for an explanation that: • The modal verb (might) in the second sentence indicates that it is possible that they will become champions but that it is not certain, which is suggested in the first sentence.	1

Spelling

You will need to help your child carry out the spelling tests.

Read out the following instruction to your child:

I am going to read the sentences to you. Each sentence has a word missing. Listen carefully to the missing word and fill in the answer space, making sure that you spell the missing word correctly.
First I will read the word, then the word within the sentence, then I will repeat the word a third time.

You should now read the spellings three times, as given below. Leave at least a 12-second gap between spellings. At the end, read all the sentences again, giving your child the chance to make any changes they wish to their answers.

Question	Spelling	Mark
Spelling Test 1		
1	The word is **know**. *They did not* ***know*** *where they were going.* The word is **know.**	1
2	The word is **mechanic**. *The* ***mechanic*** *checked their car.* The word is **mechanic**.	1
3	The word is **sensation**. *When she closed her eyes, she got a strange* ***sensation****.* The word is **sensation**.	1
4	The word is **directly**. *Jasmin was told to go* ***directly*** *to the school office.* The word is **directly**.	1

5	The word is **roughest**. *The oldest whale had the* ***roughest*** *skin.* The word is **roughest**.	1
6	The word is **beginning**. *It was* ***beginning*** *to get colder as winter approached.* The word is **beginning**.	1
7	The word is **information**. *The* ***information*** *was useful to the police.* The word is **information**.	1
8	The word is **comfortable**. *They were the most* ***comfortable*** *shoes she could find.* The word is **comfortable**.	1
Spelling Test 2		
1	The word is **forgotten**. *We had all* ***forgotten*** *the words to the song.* The word is **forgotten**.	1
2	The word is **sadly**. *They waved* ***sadly*** *as the train left the platform.* The word is **sadly**.	1
3	The word is **curious**. *Jenny knew there was something* ***curious*** *about the old clock.* The word is **curious**.	1
4	The word is **crescent**. *A beautiful* ***crescent*** *moon hung in the night sky.* The word is **crescent**.	1
5	The word is **special**. *The kindness of others had made the day* ***special****.* The word is **special**.	1
6	The word is **sensible**. *Wearing a hat was a* ***sensible*** *decision.* The word is **sensible**.	1
7	The word is **cough**. *His* ***cough*** *kept him awake all night.* The word is **cough**.	1
8	The word is **herd**. *The farmer had a huge* ***herd*** *of cattle.* The word is **herd**.	1
Spelling Test 3		
1	The word is **young**. *It was a very* ***young*** *whale they spotted.* The word is **young**.	1
2	The word is **famous**. *There was a statue of a* ***famous*** *actress.* The word is **famous**.	1
3	The word is **television**. *They could find nothing to watch on* ***television****.* The word is **television**.	1
4	The word is **echo**. *Jack heard his voice* ***echo*** *around the cave.* The word is **echo**.	1
5	The word is **confident**. *They were* ***confident*** *they would win the race.* The word is **confident**.	1
6	The word is **reliable**. *The car had always been very* ***reliable****.* The word is **reliable**.	1
7	The word is **through**. *Everybody squeezed* ***through*** *the gap in the fence.* The word is **through**.	1
8	The word is **recognise**. *Nobody would* ***recognise*** *her in this disguise.* The word is **recognise**.	1
Spelling Test 4		
1	The word is **double**. *There were* ***double*** *yellow lines on the road.* The word is **double**.	1
2	The word is **submarine**. *He explored the ocean floor in a* ***submarine****.* The word is **submarine**.	1
3	The word is **picture**. *He painted a* ***picture*** *of the mountain.* The word is **picture**.	1
4	The word is **medal**. *Each runner received a* ***medal*** *and certificate.* The word is **medal**.	1
5	The word is **possible**. *Anything is* ***possible*** *with the right attitude.* The word is **possible**.	1
6	The word is **ceiling**. *Cobwebs hung from the* ***ceiling*** *in the old ballroom.* The word is **ceiling**.	1
7	The word is **vehicle**. *A special* ***vehicle*** *was needed to cross the river.* The word is **vehicle**.	1
8	The word is **muscle**. *She pulled a* ***muscle*** *but still scored the goal.* The word is **muscle**.	1
Spelling Test 5		
1	The word is **gardening**. *The whole family loved* ***gardening****.* The word is **gardening**.	1
2	The word is **misbehave**. *The pupils were asked to not* ***misbehave****.* The word is **misbehave**.	1
3	The word is **various**. *The menu contained* ***various*** *fish dishes.* The word is **various**.	1
4	The word is **angrily**. *A ball was thrown* ***angrily*** *in their direction.* The word is **angrily**.	1
5	The word is **decision**. *It was a tough* ***decision*** *to make.* The word is **decision**.	1
6	The word is **magician**. *The* ***magician*** *needed much more practice.* The word is **magician**.	1

7	The word is **chorus**. *They all knew the **chorus** so joined in.* The word is **chorus**.	1
8	The word is **adorable**. *Sam had never seen such **adorable** kittens.* The word is **adorable**.	1
Spelling Test 6		
1	The word is **myth**. *Charlie enjoyed reading the **myth** about the moor.* The word is **myth**.	1
2	The word is **beginner**. *Annie was a great violinist for a **beginner**.* The word is **beginner**.	1
3	The word is **division**. *Long **division** is often quite challenging.* The word is **division**.	1
4	The word is **serious**. *A **serious** incident was reported to the police.* The word is **serious**.	1
5	The word is **league**. *The school netball team won the **league**.* The word is **league**.	1
6	The word is **ambitious**. *The scientist had always been **ambitious**.* The word is **ambitious**.	1
7	The word is **horribly**. *The creature made some **horribly** rude noises.* The word is **horribly**.	1
8	The word is **doubt**. *There was no **doubt** that this was a great day.* The word is **doubt**.	1
Spelling Test 7		
1	The word is **country**. *It was a fascinating **country** to visit.* The word is **country**.	1
2	The word is **enough**. *It was not windy **enough** to fly a kite.* The word is **enough**.	1
3	The word is **treasure**. *They were promised great **treasure** by the goblin.* The word is **treasure**.	1
4	The word is **machine**. *They built a magnificent **machine** from junk.* The word is **machine**.	1
5	The word is **jealous**. *Everyone was a little **jealous** of his amazing voice.* The word is **jealous**.	1
6	The word is **mist**. *An icy **mist** suspended itself over the lake.* The word is **mist**.	1
7	The word is **incredible**. *Penguins are **incredible** at swimming.* The word is **incredible**.	1
8	The word is **thorough**. *They were very **thorough** in their research.* The word is **thorough**.	1
Spelling Test 8		
1	The word is **thought**. *I **thought** it was raining outside.* The word is **thought**.	1
2	The word is **imagine**. *It was hard to **imagine** how it used to look.* The word is **imagine**.	1
3	The word is **strange**. *There was a **strange** noise coming from the car.* The word is **strange**.	1
4	The word is **basically**. *They were **basically** stuck until help arrived.* The word is **basically**.	1
5	The word is **knot**. *A large **knot** was used to hold the rope in place.* The word is **knot**.	1
6	The word is **opportunity**. *It was an **opportunity** to visit a new place.* The word is **opportunity**.	1
7	The word is **shoulder**. *She hurt her **shoulder** when she fell off the bike.* The word is **shoulder**.	1
8	The word is **neighbour**. *Yesterday we got a new **neighbour**.* The word is **neighbour**.	1

Score Chart

You have completed all the tests! Now write your scores in the score chart below.

Test	My Score
Arithmetic Test 1	/13
Arithmetic Test 2	/14
Arithmetic Test 3	/13
Arithmetic Test 4	/13
Arithmetic Test 5	/13
Arithmetic Test 6	/14
Arithmetic Test 7	/13
Arithmetic Test 8	/12
Reasoning Test 1	/13
Reasoning Test 2	/14
Reasoning Test 3	/13
Reasoning Test 4	/12
Reasoning Test 5	/13
Reasoning Test 6	/12
Reasoning Test 7	/14
Reasoning Test 8	/12
Reading Test 1	/9
Reading Test 2	/9
Reading Test 3	/9
Reading Test 4	/9
Reading Test 5	/9

Test	My Score
Reading Test 6	/9
Reading Test 7	/9
Reading Test 8	/9
G and P Test 1	/11
G and P Test 2	/11
G and P Test 3	/11
G and P Test 4	/11
G and P Test 5	/11
G and P Test 6	/11
G and P Test 7	/11
G and P Test 8	/11
Spelling Test 1	/8
Spelling Test 2	/8
Spelling Test 3	/8
Spelling Test 4	/8
Spelling Test 5	/8
Spelling Test 6	/8
Spelling Test 7	/8
Spelling Test 8	/8
Total	**/432**

How did you do?

I did brilliantly!
Fabulous!

I did well.
Great stuff!

I did ok.
Well done – keep up the practice if you want to improve.

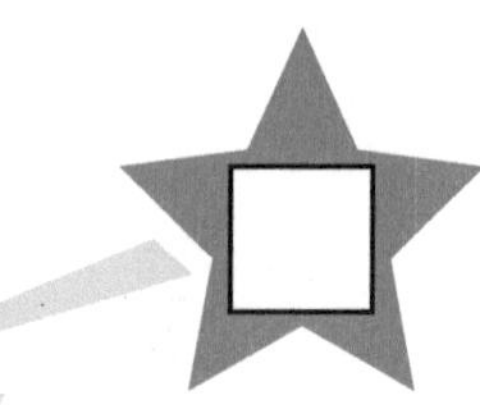

I didn't do so well.
Don't worry – there's still time to learn and practise. Why not try these tests again?